Lallā to Nūruddīn

Lallā to Nūruddīn

Rishī-Sufi Poetry of Kashmir

A Translation and Study

Jaishree K. Odin

MOTILAL BANARSIDASS PUBLISHERS
PRIVATE LIMITED • DELHI (INDIA)

Reprint: Delhi, 2016
First Edition: Delhi, 2013

ISBN: 978-81-208-3690-7

MOTILAL BANARSIDASS
41 U.A. Bungalow Road, Jawahar Nagar, Delhi 110 007
8 Mahalaxmi Chamber, 22 Bhulabhai Desai Road, Mumbai 400 026
203 Royapettah High Road, Mylapore, Chennai 600 004
236, 9th Main III Block, Jayanagar, Bengaluru 560 011
8 Camac Street, Kolkata 700 017
Ashok Rajpath, Patna 800 004
Chowk, Varanasi 221 001

Printed in India

by RP Jain at NAB Printing Unit,
A-44, Naraina Industrial Area, Phase I, New Delhi–110028
and published by JP Jain for Motilal Banarsidass Publishers (P) Ltd,
41 U.A. Bungalow Road, Jawahar Nagar, Delhi-110007

Contents

Preface

In the spring of 2007, I returned briefly to the land of my birth to do preliminary research on the Rishī Sufis of Kashmir. I was filled with apprehension about going back to the Valley from which all my near and dear relatives had left due to political disturbance in the 1990s. Although I got off from the airplane at Srinagar airport with some uneasiness, what transpired over the next twenty-four hours resolved all my apprehensions about this undertaking. I was taken from the airport to the outskirts of the city to visit an outstanding and highly respected Sufi—the result of an introduction over the phone by a relative in Delhi, who described me as a scholar on Lallā (14th century Kashmiri Śaiva poet), now doing research on Nūruddīn Rishī. As I entered the sitting room of the Sufi, I was amazed to see members of both communities, Hindus and Muslims. And later on I heard from the Sufi himself that it is the intellect that divides people into discrete communities and it is love that unites them. The whole family, three generations living under one roof, opened their hearts and home to me. My interaction with the local people over the next seven days convinced me that the Rishī Sufis might have ceased to be a distinct order centuries ago, but their spirit, embodied in the commonly used expression *kashmiriyat*, signifying the unique Kashmiri tradition of religious syncretism and communal harmony, associated with Nūruddīn Rishī and his senior contemporary Śaiva poet Lallā, is still alive and well in the twenty-first century in many sections of society in the Valley.

Nūruddīn Rishī (1378–1439), also known as Nund Rishī or Shaikh Nūruddīn, founded the indigenous Sufi order of Muslim Rishīs in the beginning of the fifteenth century in the midst of intensified activities of the missionary Sufis from Central Asia and Persia. Rooted in the Islamic tradition, the Rishī Sufis integrated local customs and traditions into their teachings, which differentiated them from the immigrant Sufis and their Kashmiri followers. People were attracted to Rishī Sufis not only due to their elevated spiritual status, but also because their lives were based on ethical values of non-violence, religious tolerance, and compassion for the poor and the needy. They spread the message of peaceful coexistence of all people irrespective of their caste, class, or religious creed and they contributed to creating a tradition of communal harmony, which became an integral part of the Kashmiri culture for centuries. The order was active with a distinct identity for about two hundred years before becoming absorbed in the mainstream Sufism. Even though it has ceased to be a distinct order with its own identity, many Sufi mystics in the Valley continue to embody the spirit of the Rishī Sufis, as they too believe in religious tolerance, compassion, and peaceful coexistence. However, the Rishī Sufi worldview is "hidden" or "suppressed" due to increasingly orthodox elements in the Kashmiri society. We need to unearth this narrative and acknowledge its silent presence in some contemporary urban and rural spaces of the Valley. The present study and translation of Nūruddīn Rishī's verses are an attempt to contribute in this direction.

I thank the University of Hawai'i's Research Relations Office that awarded me a grant to travel to India to do preliminary research on Rishī Sufis in the spring of 2007. I especially thank the Fulbright Association for the senior Fulbright Research Fellowship during the 2008–09 academic year that funded my sabbatical research on Rishī Sufis in India. I am also grateful to the Jamia Milia Islamia University, New Delhi, and the University of Kashmir, Srinagar, which provided me the research facilities during my stay in India. For conversations that enriched my understanding of different perspectives on the Sufi traditions of India in general, and of Kashmir in particular, my many thanks go to Professors Akhtarul Wasey, Shafi Shauq, Majrooh Rashid, Lily Want, Latif Kazmi, and Sanaullah Mir, and my research assistant Naseem Gul. My special thanks go to Ajaz Anwar Pirzada, who in the summer of 2011 went over each single verse with me to check if I had translated it correctly. In addition, I wish to thank the Mir family, especially Tabassum Mir, whose hospitality during the multiple visits I made to Srinagar between 2007 and 2011 made me feel that I had indeed returned home. I must above all gratefully acknowledge Jawahar Wattal, who introduced me to the great Sufi mystic of Kashmir Rahman Sahib, without whose guidance this book would never have seen the light of the day. Rahman Sahib has been my mentor and guide as I grappled with the intricate maze of Sufi metaphysics to understand the moral and ecological vision of Rishī Sufis of Kashmir. It is through him that I have learned the true spirit of Rishī Sufism, which has been a part of Kashmiri culture for centuries. To Rahman Sahib I dedicate this book for his love, compassion, and enormous generosity of spirit.

Introduction

Kashmir became the home of foreign missionaries from Persia and Central Asia during the fourteenth century. The activities of foreign missionaries intensified after Muslim rule was solidified with the establishment of the Shah Mir dynasty in 1339 that ruled Kashmir for about two hundred years. As Suhrawardī and Kubravī Sufi missionaries and their Kashmiri followers preached the new faith to the local people, an indigenous Sufi movement emerged in the countryside in the first decades of the fifteenth century under the leadership of Nūruddīn Rishī, who is also known as Nund Rishī or Shaikh Nūruddīn. Rishī Sufis lived austere and devout lives and worked toward the betterment of humanity by spreading the message of love, peace, and simple living.

In *Ā'in-i Akbarī*, a 16th century Mughal chronicle, Abu'l-Fazl describes Rishī Sufis as the "most respected class of people" in Kashmir who had not "abandoned the traditional and customary forms of worship," but they were "true in their worship." They did "not denounce men belonging to different faiths," and they observed celibacy, abstained from meat, and planted fruit bearing trees.[1] The Mughal emperor Jahāngīr (1605–1627) in his memoirs corroborates Abu'l-Fazl's account and describes Muslim Rishīs as simple, unpretentious people, who did not marry, who did not consume meat, and who planted fruit-bearing trees in uninhabited places so others may enjoy the fruit.[2] The hagiographical accounts from the medieval period further reveal the lifestyle and worldview of the Rishīs. Baba Dāwud Khākī, a Suhrawardī saint, comments in his *Rishī Nāmā*

---

[1] *Ā'in-i Akbarī II*, p. 170, quoted in Rafiqi, pp. 236–237.

[2] *Tūzuk-i-Jahāngīrī*, trans. Rogers and Beveridge, vol. II, pp. 149–150, quoted in Sufi, vol. I, p. 97.

(1580–81) that "a Rishī is one who is an ascetic, is disciplined, and leads a life different from other saints. He is free from all worldly pleasures."[3] Baba Nasīb in his *Rishī Nāmā* (1631–32) describes Rishīs as "men of pure heart," who withdrew completely from the worldly life, fasting incessantly during the day and devoting their nights to worship.[4] Bahāuddīn Mattū (1832) in his account notes that Rishī Sufis were famous "for their devotion to Divine Unity and for killing their carnal desires. Although they retire[d] to caves, they illuminate[d] them with the light of their spiritual attainment."[5]

Rishī Sufis lived in the countryside. They usually did not have any formal education and they refused to have anything to do with the royal court or the administration. They helped the needy and the sick and refrained from inflicting injury on any living beings. They believed in peaceful coexistence and tolerance of other religions. Hardi Rishī, a distinguished Rishī, is reported to have said: "We are not bigots and that Rishīs do not cause pain."[6] Rishī Sufis were thus unassuming and acted with humility, patience, and fortitude. They were anchored in the local traditions and customs and they lived exceedingly austere and devout lives. Many people converted to Islam under their influence because they saw commonality between their own worldview and those of Rishīs.

Several historical studies on the role of Muslim Rishīs in the spread of Islam in Kashmir have appeared in recent years. In *Kashmir's Transition to Islam* (1994), Ishaq Khan comments on the integration of local customs and traditions in Rishī thought, which was critical to Islam's appeal to the Kashmiri masses in medieval times. He, however, describes the syncretic religious worldview of Rishīs only as a passing

---

[3] Khākī, *Rishī Nāmā*, ff. 8b–9a, 66b, quoted in Rafiqi, p. 237.
[4] Nasīb, *Rishī Nāmā*, f. 127a–b, see Rafiqi, pp. 238–239.
[5] Mattū, *Rishī Nāmā*, f. 10a–b, quoted in Rafiqi, p. 239.
[6] Khākī, *Rishī Nāmā*, f. 11b, quoted in Rafiqi, p. 241.

marker to the orthodox versions of Sharia-based Islam. In *Islam in Kashmir* (2004), Wani takes a diametrically opposite view in that he emphasizes the role of the missionary Sufi movements in medieval Kashmir in the spread of Islam, relegating the role of Muslim Rishīs to the background. Wani describes Sufi missionaries as the representatives of the civilization-building cultures of Central Asia and Persia, thereby ignoring the historical fact that Kashmir was a region of sophisticated philosophical speculation (Buddhism and Śaivism) and artistic expression until the twelfth century. In *Sufism in Kashmir* (2001), Rafiqi provides yet another perspective for understanding the role of Muslim Rishīs. He sees the spread of Islam in medieval Kashmir in terms of two streams of thought: the Muslim Rishī movement and the immigrant Sufi movement. The primary aim of immigrant Sufis was to preach Islam. They were mostly attached to the royal court and worked to spread Islam from above unlike the Rishī Sufis, who were active in the countryside amongst the rural people and taught in the native tongue. Rishī Sufis were anchored in the local tradition and showed tolerance towards other religions. They were "sympathetic towards all living creatures and condemned tyranny and violence of all kinds."[7]

Though Rafiqi gives Muslim Rishīs their own unique identity, he too does not bring out their relevance for contemporary times. The reason for this omission is that historical analysis of the Rishī movement, though important, has its limitations, as it only deals with the historical facts about the evolution of the Islamic ideology in Kashmir over the last six centuries or the dynamics of interactions between various streams of Sufi orders as they established themselves in the Valley in medieval times. Such details do not engage the esoteric dimensions of the Rishī phenomena to explore why it has and continues to be, though covertly, an integral

[7] Rafiqi, p. 248.

part of the Kashmiri imagination. When examined as a body, the current scholarship produces a fragmented view of the contemporary significance of Rishī Sufis. An undue stress is laid on establishing links between the Rishī Sufi tradition and the immigrant Sufi orders in order to integrate Rishī Sufis into the broader history of Islam in Kashmir. Undoubtedly, such historical studies have a place in the Rishī scholarship. However, reducing the significance of the movement to its historical relevance in the history of the spread of Islam undermines the universal message of Muslim Rishīs that makes it so unique in the cultural history of Kashmir.

The word "Rishi" or "Ṛsi" in Sanskrit generally means a "sage" or an "enlightened person." Some medieval Muslim writers have seen it as a derivation of the Persian word *Raish* or *Rish*, which means feathers of a bird or wings, though later Muslim writers have accepted the Sanskrit origin of the word. Baba Dāwud Mishkātī (a 17th century Suhrawardī Sufi saint) writes that Rishīs were in existence in Kashmir from ancient times, but Nūruddīn Rishī islamized the local ascetic tradition of Rishīs.[8] The fact that "a strong folk tradition still persists, particularly in a number of villages of Kashmir, about the existence of Rishīs in ancient times, and that some forests in the Valley are even named after them gives a certain degree of credence to the oral sources of the Rishī tradition."[9] The ancient anchorite and ascetic tradition of Nāth Yogis in India was preserved in both Śaiva and Buddhist ascetic practices of Kashmir and the surrounding Himalayan region. This tradition rejected external worship of idols using ritual objects; instead, it advocated renunciation to achieve an inward directed mind through mental visualization and breathing practices. As in the Sufi tradition, the teacher-to-disciple transmission was

[8] Mishkātī, *Asrāru'l-Abrār*, f. 53a–b, see Rafiqi, p. 161.
[9] Khan, p. 36.

an integral part of this tradition. Nūruddīn, a Sufi mystic, and his senior contemporary Lallā, a Śaiva mystic, both drew on this local oral Rishī tradition. It is for this reason perhaps that their poetic output, in so far as it reveals a specific moral vision, shows considerable similarities. It is again for this reason that their lives are so intertwined in the Kashmiri cultural imagination. Both promoted love, non-violence, religious tolerance, and the need for self-transformation in search of One God. As Lallā's verses became a part of the cultural repertoire of medieval Kashmir and Nūruddīn Rishī revered her greatly, it is important to give a brief overview of the legacy that she left behind.

Lallā's Legacy

Lallā was born in Kashmir sometime in the early 1300s and she died in the 1370s or 1380s. She was married into a Brahmin family of Pāmpor at a young age. Legends speak about her mother-in-law as a tyrant, who filled her married life with suffering. Her husband also ill-treated her. She suffered silently as she quietly devoted herself to spiritual practice, into which she was initiated by Siddha Śri Kanṭh. When she could no longer endure the ill-treatment at home, she renounced her family.

Lallā's aphoristic verses have been an integral part of the Kashmiri culture for centuries. The oral transmission of her compositions over a prolonged period of time illustrates the extent to which she has been a part of the folk memory. In spite of being such an integral part of the Kashmiri language and culture, she was left out of the Sanskrit literature of the following centuries. The primary reason for this neglect could have been that the Sanskrit chronicles focused mainly on kings and the political intrigues surrounding them. She, however, lived in the countryside and it was the common people who treasured her verses, which made her a part of the Kashmiri folk imagination rather than the elite brahminical tradition. The earliest reference to Lallā is in Baba Dāwud Mishkātī's *Asrāru'l-Abrār,* a hagiographic account completed in 1652–53.[10] Mishkātī describes her as Lallā 'Ārifa, an advanced mystic, and relates the water pitcher legend about her, which marks the time when she renounced her home and became an ascetic.[11] Lallā's critique of social and religious institutions of her time and early references to her in the Persian hagiographic documents and chronicles have led a few scholars to conclude that she either adopted Sufi mysticism, or was influenced by it, or she brought about its synthesis with Hinduism.[12] Recent scholars have refuted such claims based on the study of either the Persian sources or the content of verses or both.[13]

Lallā's verses, originally uttered in the old Kashmiri, are filled with vivid images that capture thoughts and experiences of her life. Some verses deal with the beginning of her quest as she struggles to discipline her body and mind. Others specifically focus on her experiences with sustained introspective contemplation. In the third group of verses, she turns her attention outwards and takes on the role of a

---

[10] Kaul (1973), p. 2.

[11] According to the legend, Lallā got up before dawn every day and walked to the river in a nearby village to fetch a pitcher of water. Instead of filling the pitcher with water and directly returning home, she would visit a shrine across the river to meditate. One morning her husband quietly followed her to the river bank to find out why she took so long to return home. He was filled with anger at her diversion. That day when Lalla returned home with the earthen pitcher full of water on her head, her husband hit the pitcher with his stick; the pitcher broke into pieces, but the water stayed miraculously intact on her head. Lalla calmly went inside the house, poured the water into smaller vessels, throwing the left-over water outside. From this water, a pond was formed, which became known as the Pond of Lallā. This incident marks the time of her renunciation when she left her family and became a wandering ascetic.

[12] Temple, 1924; Hasan, 1959; Bazaz, 1959; Bamzai 1962; and Sufi, 1974.

[13] Rafiqi, 1972; Kaul, 1973; and Odin, 1999.

teacher to instruct others how to free themselves from worldly attachments and lead a disciplined life, engaged in self-transformation and the transformation of their community.[14]

As Lallā begins her quest, she describes the worldly life in terms of a river, which she needs to cross in order to reach the other shore. She prepares herself psychologically and physically for the journey as she finds herself adrift in the material world, where everything is subject to death. In a verse, she compares her body to a house and her sense organs to its doors and windows that must be kept shut in order for her to stay focused on her practice. The "mind-horse" needs to be brought under control to experience the higher Self. The following verse poignantly reflects her effort to tear herself away from the comforts and pleasures of life by reminding herself of their transitory nature:[15]

I gently lament for you.
Mind, you are in love with illusion.
Not a shadow of this worldly splendor
  will accompany you.
Oh, why do you forget your real nature? (Kak, 2007, v. 5)

She burns the "impurities of the heart" and kills her "desires" as she surrenders completely. Intense yearning and love, she realizes, are necessary to cultivate to get closer to the object of her quest. She "suffers the fire of love" as she awakens the Beloved within her. She conveys the experience of "awakening her darling" by using vivid images of "grinding" the heart in the "mortar of love," and "burning" and "roasting" it and "tasting" it herself.

---

[14] For a detailed discussion of Lallā's verses, see Kak, pp. 1–20 & pp. 193–213.

[15] All quoted verses of Lallā in this section are from *Mystical Verses of Lallā* trans. J. Kak, Delhi, 2007.

I ground my heart in the mortar of love.
Evil thoughts left me and I became calm.
I burned and roasted it and tasted it myself.
How do I know if this practice will
  let me live or die? (Kak, 2007, v. 18)

In yet another verse, she says:

Impurities of my mind were
  wiped away as from a mirror,
    and I attained self-knowledge.
I saw Him near me—
He is everything and
  I am nothing. (Kak, 2007, v. 68)

Lallā addressed her verses to people in the countryside. Accordingly, some of her verses speak about the need for devotion to Śiva or God, others describe Him as the transcendental reality that permeates the physical reality, and yet others focus on the need to do away entirely with duality of all kinds in order to find a totally new space for the actualizing self. The ultimate goal in this handful of verses, then, is to go beyond the meditation and the object of meditation and reach a state that transcends thought constructs of all kinds.

Neither you nor I,
  and neither meditation
    nor the object of meditation exist.
The All doer forgets Himself.
The blind find this meaningless.
The wise become one
  with this supreme state. (Kak, 2007, v. 61)

The underlying current of Lallā's experiences is best represented by those verses that portray God as the transcendental reality, which is beyond any anthropomorphic representation, a reality that goes beyond subject-object duality since it is the essential ground of both. The difficult task that Lallā faces is how to represent this reality using language that always objectifies what it represents. Finally, she describes this state by simply saying what it is not. Lallā speaks about this final state in terms of nothingness coming in touch with nothingness. The notion of nothingness (*śūnya*) in her verses is not in negative or nihilistic terms. Instead, it represents a space that cannot be contained in any dualistic categories. The experience of nothingness is a mystic experience. The metaphor of touch can be used to understand the experience in which the relationship between the finite consciousness and the universal consciousness is not of indifferential identity, but rather of an unfolding of the unity, where each state has its own reality.[16]

Even though leading the life of an ascetic, Lallā is very much concerned about the welfare of people and her verses are a living testimony to that fact. She urges people to control greed, anger, and desire by exercising self-restraint and engaging in good deeds. Thus, she says:

Kill your mortal enemies—
  lust, anger, and desire.
Otherwise they would kill you
  with their arrows.
Calm them with self restraint
  and good thoughts.
Recognize their nature
  and their power. (Kak, 2007, v. 134)

The desire for material things and experiences is a major source of misery in this world. One way to overcome the appetite for material things, according to Lallā, is by focusing on their transitoriness. She reminds people not to be preoccupied with their body and its desire for pleasurable

[16] For a detailed discussion of Lallā's relationship to the Kashmir Śaiva tradition, see Kak, pp. 193–213.

experiences as "not even dust and ashes will remain of this body" (Kak, 2007, v. 139). In a verse, she says

> Acquiring a kingdom
>   will not make you content.
> Renouncing it
>   will not satisfy your mind.
> Free from desires,
>   you will not die.
> Self-knowledge is to be dead
>   to worldly things while still alive. (Kak, 2007, v. 133)

Lallā critiques the prescriptive religious practices of all kinds. Thus, renouncing home in itself is not enough to come closer to God and neither is reciting prayers, chanting mantras, or turning rosary beads. Performing habitually religious practices might give the individual satisfaction of engaging in something spiritual, but, in reality, would do nothing to expand their limited vision to bring them closer to God. Similarly, objects of ritual worship, for example, kuśa grass, sesame seeds, lamp, and water, are unnecessary, as is making an offering of animals to idols. While commenting on the goat sacrifice done in those days to appease gods and goddesses, Lallā says, it is foolish to give offerings of living creatures to dead stones (idols); goats live on grass and water and their wool covers our bodies, keeping us warm. She thus advises people to cultivate compassion and refrain from killing or injuring any living being.

The real religious practice, Lallā says, lies in deliberate self-introspection that involves not only controlling one's mind and one's breath, but also renouncing negative character traits and performing good deeds that benefit others. For Lallā, aquiring knowlegde and opening up to the divine consciousness is a living act, which requires inner transformation. It is thus different from a religious scholar's accumulation of intellectual knowledge. In one of her verses she says that she learned some things from books, but others she learned through direct experience. Thus, she emphasizes direct experience above any elaborate study of texts. She is critical of the Brahmin elite who take great pride in their scholarly achievement. However, their scholarship does not necessarily mean that they have true insight into the subject they write about.

As a wandering ascetic, Lallā relies on the food offered to her by others, who belong to a community other than her own. In the following verse, she critiques the social practices of her time when the upper caste Hindus did not consider the food cooked by Muslims or by Hindus of lower castes clean enough to be consumed.

I renounced
 falsehood, deceit, and hypocrisy.
I told my mind to follow this teaching.
Only One I found in everyone—
 What is wrong with eating with anyone? (Kak, 2007, v. 121)

In yet another verse, she says:

The world is full of differences.
If you are tolerant,
 you will be happy.
If you renounce anger, hate, and animosity,
 you will see Śiva's face. (Kak, 2007, v. 146)

Lallā thus preaches tolerance towards religions other than one's own. Even though people might belong to a different caste or religious creed, they are all sustained by the same divine consciousness, which is like the bright sun that shines equally everywhere. It is the clouds of ignorance, according to Lallā, that stop the ever present illumination. Once the clouds disappear, the divine consciousness reveals itself pervading both the visible and the invisible world. In a verse, she elaborates on this idea by referring to the single source of stones that serve various functions. Some stones, she says, serve as parts of the grinding stone, a tool for grinding wheat that nourishes the body, and others adorn the temple altars where people go to fulfill their spiritual needs. Still others are used for building pavements for people to tread upon. Yet all types of stones come from the earth. Similarly, the source of diversity in the world is the same Ultimate Reality or God, even as different created beings or things follow their own arc of being and becoming in the world. Hence, Lallā refrains from identifying herself with any caste or religious creed. God as the Ultimate Reality is beyond any artificial divisions. People might call this state Śiva, Keśava, Mahāvīr, or Buddha, but these are just different names assigned to the same reality.

The Self may be named Śiva,
  Keśava, or Mahāvīr
    or the lotus born Buddha.
Whatever name it may have,
  may it set free a weakling like me
    from worldly afflictions. (Kak, 2007, v. 12)

In yet another verse, she urges people not to discriminate between Hindus and Muslims:

Śiva is omnipresent.
Don't differentiate between
  Hindus and Muslims.
If you are wise, you will recognize
  your true Self—
That is your real acquaintance
  with the Lord. (Kak, 2007, v. 83)

Many of Lallā's verses focus on the need to cultivate one's character to make progress on the spiritual path as negative character traits strengthen the ego and its constant preoccupation with satisfying worldly desires. She urges people to change from within and manifest that change in their actions by performing good deeds with detachment. She brings people's attention to the need for a personal morality based on honesty and responsibility rather than on rules of conduct based on religious bigotry. In a verse, she says:

Responsibility for your actions
  you must bear—
Others share their fruits.
Without attachment,
  I offer my actions to the higher Self.
Wherever I go is all right with me. (Kak, 2007, v. 84)

Lallā's emphasis on religious and social equality, as testified in her verses, shows that she was quite secular in her outlook, which is perhaps the reason why she has been held in such high reverence by Hindus and Muslims alike. It can be said that Lallā's intense concern for people, as reflected in many of her verses, was to a great extent shaped by the missionary outlook of the Sufis. But one could also say that Lallā drew on the local Rishi tradition that had absorbed the practices of Buddhist ascetics and Nāth yogis, who saw themselves as outsiders to the high culture, which was dominated by elaborate and complicated rituals and caste politics. The free mingling of Sufi and Śaiva mystics during her time resulted in their appreciation of genuine spiritual experience over religious dogmas of any kind.

Nūruddīn and the local Rishī tradition

As has been shown by scholars, mysticism is common to all religions and it focuses on the experience of the Oneness of God. Mystic experiences can thus be had within the context of one's own religious framework, even as the experiences belonging to different traditions show commonalities. Nūruddīn traces his lineage to various Rishīs, including

Zalak, Palās, Rumi, and Mīrān (v. 53). He describes Zalak Rishī of the Ḍanḍak forest as an ascetic, who survived on wild shrubs and who had self-realization. Mīrān Rishī "lived for a thousand lunar months" and "without duality, he went to heaven" (vv. 21, 22).

No historical information is available on any of the above-named Rishīs. They were probably forest ascetics, as in medieval times it was common for ascetics to retire to forests to perform austerities. Even as Nūruddīn's worldview was deeply shaped by the local ascetic practices, his verses reflect his belief in hell and heaven, the role of the Prophet, and the resurrection. The Rishī Sufi tradition, discussed at length in the next section, was above all a mystic Islamic movement, which was based on cardinal principles of asceticism, vegetarianism, and celibacy.

The themes that stand out in Nūruddīn's verses pertain to death, mortality, communion with God, world as a community, non-violence, and universal love. Both immigrant Sufi and Muslim Rishī saints were rooted in the Islamic tradition, but it was only the Rishī order that retained the local traditions and customs of extreme asceticism, vegetarianism, and one-pointed devotion to God. For this, they were criticized by the immigrant Sufis. All mystic traditions postulate that mystic experience is only possible through intuition and not through intellectual or sensory perception. Hence, mystics turn their attention inwards through withdrawing the senses from the external world so the inner world opens up in its fullness. The austerities and penance are an important aspect of purification of the body and soul in many mystic traditions. Those studies that are apologetic about this aspect of Muslim Rishīs fail to see its significance in the mystical journey of the Rishīs and how it fits in with similar tendencies of many famous medieval Sufis in India, especially of the Chistī order in the thirteenth and fourteenth centuries in India, or even with the broader Islamic world in the formative stages of Sufism.

In order to understand the relationship between the indigenous Rishī Sufi tradition and the immigrant Sufi orders in medieval Kashmir, it is important to point out that the basic mission of the immigrant Sufis was to preach Islam. They were proficient in Arabic and Persian and were usually attached to the royal court and thus belonged to the high culture. They looked down upon the unlettered or semi-literate Rishīs, who lived in the countryside, who did not know any Arabic or Persian, and who spread their message using the local Kashmiri dialect, which for the immigrant Sufis was the language of illiterate people. The immigrant Sufis and their Kashmiri followers openly criticized the severe ascetic practices of Nūruddīn and his followers, which they believed were not aligned with the laws of the Shariah. The missionary Sufis thus had a different perception of the fundamental emphasis of the Koran and the Sunnah of Muhammad. They stressed the role of the Shariah in individual life and social responsibilities toward God. From a theological perspective, their religious vision was guided by the transcendent form of God, which is incomparable and inaccessible.

Nūruddīn Rishī, however, perceived his religion in terms of his inner relationship to God through love, and thus he emphasized the loving and gentle face of God as expressed in the well-known prophetic saying or hadith, "God's mercy takes precedence over His wrath." He and his followers preferred seclusion to interaction with worldly people, though they were actively engaged in helping people who sought their guidance. Non-Muslims were attracted to Rishīs "since they seem to have perceived little difference between the goals pursued by them and by the Muslim Rishīs."[17] In their interaction, Rishī Sufis showed humility and loving care for the other, which is reflected in Nūruddīn's statement: "I neither bear any prejudice to someone nor do I try to outdo

[17] Khan, p. 38.

others."[18] He rejected religious dogma and orthodoxy and emphasized the transformation of character through giving up pride, jealousy, arrogance, anger, and hatred and through controlling the carnal self both in its material appetite and moral laxity. He taught by example as he lived what he preached and transmitted his teachings in the native tongue.

An interesting reading of the Rishī Sufi movement is presented by Maroof Shah, who sees the need to go beyond the exoteric dimensions of the Rishī movement as it is manifested in the Rishī lifestyle to the esoteric dimensions of Rishī thought or its metaphysical foundations to understand its relevance for contemporary times. The Rishī Sufi phenomena is not "an ideology, but it is a way of life characterized by selfless service to fellow humans and belief in dignity of life." It is an "ethical philosophy that could be practiced anywhere anytime by anyone" and it is "committed to belief in non-violence and peace." Shah further notes that the Rishī Sufis have "influenced Kashmir's religion and culture so deeply that it could well be seen as the defining creed or philosophy of Kashmir."[19] This philosophy or worldview, commonly labeled as *kashmiriyat*, has been an integral part of the Kashmiri culture for centuries and it is best embodied in the lives of the medieval Muslim Rishīs.

The narrative of religious syncretism and communal harmony (*kashmiriyat*) has come under critique in recent times by postmodern scholars who see it as the product of colonial and nationalist project of suppressing claims to difference and identity.[20] These scholars eventually do the same thing that nationalist historians did earlier, which is to seek mono-causal and reductive explanations for events in the history of Kashmir, thereby ignoring the complex nature of regional and religious identity. The political

---

[18] Mishkātī, *Asrāru'l-Abrār*, f. 68 b, quoted in Rafiqi, p. 241.
[19] Shah, p. 118.
[20] See Zutshi, pp. 16–28.

analyses of the intracommunal differences dividing the Kashmiri Muslim community from within is a valuable contribution to understand the transformations of this community in a rapidly changing political, social, religious, and economic milieu. However, in an attempt to create a uniform narrative of cultural difference, such studies selectively focus on narratives of difference and ignore those narratives that promote notions of religious identity that are inclusive in nature as they are based on universal values of love, compassion, and caring. The Rishī Sufi phenomenon is exactly such a narrative that needs to be explored in its fullness to understand why it became such an integral part of the Kashmiri consciousness for centuries and why it still continues to exist silently in different parts of the Valley.

Life and Legends

Nūruddīn Rishī founded the Rishī Sufi movement in the early fifteenth century in Kashmir. He was born in 1378[21] in Kaimuh.[22] His ancestors from both his mother's and father's side came from a Rajput family named Sanz in Kishtwar,[23] who through the vagaries of fortune were forced to leave their native land and seek a new life in Kashmir. They belonged to the profession of watchmen or the keeper of forts built by estate owners to protect their land from neighboring estates or villages.[24] Nūruddīn's father, Salār Sanz, also called Salāruddīn, accepted Islam from the hands of Saiyid Husain Simnānī, a Kubravīya preacher, who had established himself in Kulgam.[25] His mother, Sadra, too was

[21] Some medieval sources have given the year of birth as 1356–57. More recent scholarship has accepted 1377 or 1378 as the correct date of birth because it fits more closely with the accepted date of his death. See Rafiqi, p. 162, n. 14; Gauhar, p. 18.
[22] Kaimuh is forty-eight kilometers to the south of Srinagar, Kashmir.
[23] The ancient "Kashtava" is to the south-east of Kashmir.
[24] See Gauhar, pp. 17–18.
[25] Kulgam is about fifty-one kilometers south-west of Srinagar, Kashmir.

a follower of Saiyid Husain, who arranged her marriage to Salāruddīn.

According to another tradition, it was Yāsman Rishī who was instrumental in Salāruddīn's conversion to Islam. Nūruddīn's mother, Sadra, was also a follower of Yāsman Rishī. Once when the couple were visiting Yāsman Rishī, the Śaiva mystic Lallā walked in with a bouquet of flowers and presented it to Yāsman Rishī. He passed it on to Sadra and told her that she would have a son, who would inherit the spiritual knowledge of Rishīs. Soon after this incident, Nūruddīn was born.[26] However, the incident that is most often associated with Lallā's connection with Nūruddīn took place after he was born. It is said he refused to accept milk from his mother when he was born. On the third day, Lallā visited their home and took him into her arms and said: "You were not ashamed to be born, then why be ashamed of drinking"? This legend has been interpreted as Lallā acknowledging Nūruddīn as her spiritual heir.

Not much is known about Nūruddīn's childhood years and whatever exists is shrouded in legends. At a young age, Nūruddīn lost his father. He grew up with his two brothers, who tried to get him involved in their nefarious activities, but without any success. His mother wanted him to prepare for some profession. A legend relates that once she took her son to a weaver so he could try him out to be his apprentice. As Nūruddīn watched the weaver at his loom, he asked him questions. The weaver complied by providing simple explanations of how various parts of the loom worked. Nūruddīn was not satisfied with the weaver's answers as he saw embodied in the workings of the loom a metaphor for human existence. The movement of the shuttle carrying the

---

[26] Hasan (1898), vol. III, p. 114, quoted in Parimoo, p. 11. Hasan attributes the source of this information to Mulla Ahmad who was a contemporary of Nūruddīn and is believed to have written several books, which are no longer available. Also, see Sufi, *Kashir*, vol. I, pp. 98–99.

thread back and forth suggested to him the arc that humans trace as they are born, live their life, and then die. Just as the thread that is being woven comes to an end, so does the thread of human life. In the weaver's foot movements at the loom as he worked with the paddle, he saw embodied the fate of humans, who come from dust and return to dust. The weaver had enough of him and told the mother that her son was not fit for a practical craft like weaving.[27] Nūruddīn then tried his hand as an agricultural worker. It seems he was successful at that as some legends describe his work in the fields.[28] In many verses, he uses the activities of planting a crop, nurturing it, and then harvesting it as a metaphor for one's spiritual journey that involves planting the seeds of good thoughts and nurturing them by engaging in good actions in order to make progress on the path.

Nūruddīn got married to Zai at a young age. They had three children. One of them died in infancy and the other two did not survive their childhood. Around the age of thirty, he had a spiritual awakening when he left his family and children and dug out a cave in Kaimuh, where he performed extreme austerities for many years.[29] A verse exchange describes his mother begging him to leave the cave, which was infested with rats and snakes. Nūruddīn tells her that he has renounced home and has no desire to get entangled in worldly life. He wants to live in solitude and focus on his practice in order to purify himself of anger, lust, and other temptations of the five senses. His mother reminds him that she nurtured him with her own milk and that he should at least remember that and come home. According to a legend, Nūruddīn asks her to get a pot and take back the milk she

---

[27] Parimoo, pp. 33–41; Rafiqi, p. 164, n. 23.

[28] Gauhar, p. 23.

[29] Some medieval accounts, for example by Mishkātī and Wahhāb, give Nūruddīn's age at the time of his spiritual awakening as thirty years, whereas Nasīb and Mattū in their *Rishī-Nāmā-s* state Nūruddīn's age at the time to be thirty-two years. See Rafiqi, p. 166, n. 30.

fed him when he was a baby. He hits a rock nearby and milk starts oozing out.[30] Having failed to convince her son to return home, the mother is disappointed and sends her daughter-in-law to the cave. She too entreats him to return home, but, once again, he refuses. So ends his attachment to his family.

Nūṛuddīn's name has been linked to different teachers, but no particular one is seen as his direct preceptor. His name is closely associated with Lallā. But she could not have been his direct teacher as the date of her death is somewhere around the late 1370s or early 1380s, when Nūruddīn must have been a young child. It is clear, however, that he held her in great esteem and her verse sayings were a source of inspiration for him. In one of his verses, he says: "That Lallā of Padmānpura—she drank nectar by mouthfuls. She was our avatār, too." [31]

Some legends connect Nūruddīn Rishī to the Kubravī Sufi Saiyid 'Ali Hamadānī, who visited Kashmir in 1381[32] when Nūruddīn was still a child. Others link him to Saiyid 'Ali's son Mīr Muhammad, who came to Kashmir in 1393 and spent twelve years in the Valley. Nūruddīn's meeting with Mīr Muhammad is described in various biographies and chronicles. The Mīr wanted to witness Nūruddīn's spiritual status and his companions went along with him even as they saw no need to visit an illiterate and humble Kashmiri.[33] When the Mīr saw Nūruddīn, he immediately asked him why his body was so lean. The latter replied that he had renounced all desires in order to free himself from his carnal self so he is not destroyed spiritually. Mīr Muhammad then wanted to find out why he did not consume meat. Nūruddīn replied: "According to our way of life inflicting pain on any creature

---

[30] Rafiqi, p. 166, n. 32; Parimoo, pp. 64–65.

[31] See Saqi, p. 148, n.1; Afaqi, vol. 2, p. 598; Parimoo, v. 105, p. 106.

[32] *Bahāristan-i-Shāhī*, p. 34. Also, see Rafiqi, pp. 43–44.

[33] Khan, p. 163.

is unlawful, therefore, slaughter is not permissible and that which is not appropriately slaughtered is unlawful."[34] The conversation recorded in the medieval literature shows beyond doubt that the Mīr did not approve of Nūruddīn's ascetic and vegetarian lifestyle and as such, they could not have had any teacher-disciple relationship.

In recent studies, scholars have tried to forge a connection between Mīr Muhammad and Nūruddīn, and hence, between the Kubravī order and the Rishī movement based on a letter of authority, *Khat-e-Irshād,* believed to be written in 1411. Some doubt the authenticity of this document, while others believe it is a jurisprudence decree authenticating Nūruddīn Rishī's spiritual eminence by the Mīr and establishing his connection with the Kubravī order.[35] However, Mīr Muhammad left Kashmir in 1405, so it seems unlikely that a letter of authenticity would be issued by the Sultan in 1411 after the Mīr's departure. The anecdote related to the meeting between the Mīr and Nūruddīn, described in several medieval sources, shows that the two had totally different attitudes, which makes it highly unlikely that the Mīr would have issued such a letter. Another explanation that has been put forward is that the letter, if authentic, was issued to resolve some local controversy regarding Nūruddīn, with the intention to clear the matter by affirming his spiritual eminence.[36]

Scholars write that all "the earlier sources generally agree that the preceptor of Nūruddīn is not known, describing him merely as an "Uwaisī."[37] Later sources refer to Saiyid Husain as his preceptor. However, Saiyid Husain died in 1390 when Nūruddīn was only twelve years old, so he could not

[34] Mishkātī, *Asrāru'l-Abrār,* f. 263b; see also Nasīb, *Rishī-Nāmā,* f. 246a-b; Khalīl, *Rauzātu'l Riyāz,* p. 531—conversation quoted in Rafiqi, pp. 168–169.

[35] Gauhar, pp. 37–38; Khan, pp. 161, 164.

[36] See Rafiqi, pp. lvi–lvii.

[37] Rafiqi, p. 167.

have been his teacher, especially as the sources report that he had his first spiritual awakening around the age of thirty. In a verse, Nūruddīn says that his father's preceptor was Saiyid Husain, but he does not say that with respect to himself. In Baba Nasīb's hagiographical account, the relationship between Nūruddīn and Saiyid Husain is confined to that of "mutual friendship and appreciation."[38]

Verses: the Text

Nūruddīn Rishī's verse sayings (*shruk*) were orally transmitted for about two hundred years when they began to be recorded in various chronicles and hagiographical accounts of Rishīs. The important sources include the *Rishī-Nāmā* (1580–81) written by Baba Dāwud Khākī, a Suhrawardī saint. He briefly focuses on the characteristic features of the Rishī order. His disciple Baba Nasīb also wrote a *Rishī-Nāmā* (1631–32), which is a biographical work that primarily includes legendary material on the life and actvities of Rishīs, with some verse sayings of Nūruddīn. Nasīb's disciple Baba Dāwud Mishkātī wrote *Asrāru'l-Abrār* (1652–53), which focuses on the life of various saints belonging to the important Sufi orders of Kashmir, including the Rishī order. Baba Kamāl compiled *Nūr-Nāmā* in 1802, which, in a poetic form, describes the life and achievements of Nūruddīn and his disciples. It also includes an extensive collection of Nūruddīn Rishī's verses. To make the verses easier to understand, he put together in 1835 a prose version of the compilation called *Rishī-Nāmā ('Anbar Shumāmā)*. Baba Khalīl, a junior contemporary of Baba Kamāl, produced *Rauzātu'l-Riyāz* (1835), which is yet another account of Nūruddīn Rishī and his prominent disciples. Another *Rishī-Nāmā* (1832) about the life and activities of the Rishīs was produced by Bahāuddīn Mattū. Some of the

[38] Gauhar, p. 33.

later writers of the *Rishī-Nāmā-s* have relied on earlier accounts.[39]

Various minor and major collections of Nūruddīn's verses have been published in recent years. The first edited collection of Nūruddīn's Kashmiri verses in modern times was compiled from various sources by Muhammad Amin Kamil in 1966 under the title *Nūr-Nāmā.* As new verses came to light, Moti Lal Saqi put together an expanded and edited collection titled *Kulliyāt-i-Shaikhu'l-'Ālam* (1988). Assadullah Afaqi compiled yet another collection of Kashmiri verses, *T'alimāt-i-Shaikhu'l-'Ālam* (1998), which includes an Urdu translation and commentary. The only annotated scholarly translation of the verses into English appeared in 1984 by B.N. Parimoo. His collection titled *Unity in Diversity* is based on an eighteenth century manuscript compilation of Nūruddīn's verses by Mīr Abdullāh. Other minor translations of Nūruddīn's verses have appeared in both Urdu and English from time to time. The present collection of the Kashmiri verses is primarily based on a selection from Saqi's edited collection *Kulliyāt-i-Shaikhu'l-'Ālam.* I have also consulted Afaqi's *T'alimāt-i-Shaikhu'l-'Ālam* and Parimoo's *Unity in Diversity.* The verses in the present collection were selected on the basis of their thematic and stylistic connection with one another and the degree to which they were representative of the cultural and linguistic style of the time when they were uttered.

Since no original manuscript of Nūruddīn's verses from his time is available now, it is possible to make the assumption that there have been interpolations and accretions, and even some revisions, over the centuries. Scholars have commented that the authors of the *Rishī Nāmā-s* did not know Sanskrit or Kashmiri, so the transcription of specific expressions was not always accurate. They have also speculated that some of the original Sanskrit words were slowly replaced by

---

[39] See Rafiqi, pp. lxxiii–lxxvi and pp. 319–26.

Persian or Arabic words or some verses were revised, or even left out, if they did not serve the interests of those who recorded them. In spite of that, it is easy to detect in most of the verses a certain style and thematic content characteristic of Nūruddīn's poetic corpus. In later centuries, hagiographers assigned backgrounds to his verse sayings to create the context for the verses.

Inner Journey

A portrait of Nūruddīn Rishī's inner journey can be created through weaving a tapestry of the experiences recorded in his verses before he established himself as a teacher. Many of his verses deal with his struggle of being pulled in two directions, one drawing him to the worldly life and another away from it. The *nafs* or the lower self is the major actor in this struggle with the higher Self. He compares the higher Self to the fragrant wood from a sandalwood tree with healing properties and the lower self or the ego to the hard and unyielding wood of an arkhol tree, which is good for nothing. In the initial stages of his inner journey, he also compares the power of the lower self to that of a mad elephant that has crushed him underneath. He is full of despair as he experiences himself overpowered by his lower self. Its continuous hunger for material things pulls him away from his spiritual aspirations. He knows that just "one in a thousand escapes" the ego's clutches, while "all others are trampled." Thus, he says:

My ego is like a poker
  for shoveling out hot coal.
Every moment it asks for more.
My body is too weak to remember God.
Remember God I must.
As a transient guest I have come
  to the world—I have lost all. (v. 9)

To bring his lower self under control, he reflects on the transitoriness of life. He compares the progression from youth to old age to the passing of seasons from spring to winter. At the height of spring, all is beautiful and in full bloom, but spring can be tricky because it is easy to forget that it will soon race through summer to autumn and, then, to winter. Similarly, it is easy to forget in youth about old age. In youth, Nūruddīn says, he was filled with desire for beautiful things, but then old age arrived, which he compares to the "chill of a mountain glacier" and "a turbulent storm" in the mighty lake Wular when even the most fragrant and delicious rice tasted like "the unhusked grain and chaff." Thus, he says:

Filled with desires was my fair body—
beguiled by beautiful things
I spent my youth.
My experience now is like that of
the chill of a mountain glacier and
a turbulent storm in the Wular.
The robber has robbed me of all.
The fragrant rice tastes
like the unhusked grain and chaff.
A day stretches into
a year for my poor self. (v. 6)

The "robber" in the above verse is the lower self that has robbed him of good deeds he could have accumulated in his younger days, if he had not indulged in his desire for material things. As his youth fades away into the reality of old age and its infirmities, a day now stretches for him into a year. He recalls how he used to take care of his body like precious gold, but "its value did not manifest." Now he realizes that the preoccupation with the body and its needs strengthens one's identification with the ego and thereby the ground in which it is anchored, that is the material reality. The insatiable appetite of the ego, closely linked to the body and its activities, finally ends when death arrives. The reign of the body is thus short-lived, as it is taken "like a sheep to the butcher's shop." He reminds himself that he has come to this world as a guest and a day will come when "the body after being wrapped," will be "buried under two and a half yards of earth" (v. 8).

Nūruddīn compares the soul to a bird and the body to a cage. On death, the two part ways: "When life leaves, the body is reduced to dust. Dust gets mixed with dust" (v. 48). He visualizes his own dead body pale as a delicate flower. The family members lament around his dead body, but they are helpless to do anything. However, the reality of death is more complex than simply exiting the door of life. Many of his verses reflect the Koranic belief that performing good deeds results in a positive account and negative deeds lead to a negative account for an individual, which accordingly determines an afterlife of heavenly bliss or the suffering of hell. It is in the other world that he has to "collect his wages" for what he has accomplished during his lifetime in terms of good or bad deeds.

Nūruddīn disciplines his ego and he surrenders himself to the divine will. In a verse he says that he searched for God everywhere, but not a trace did he find anywhere. He even asked Mullahs and ascetics repeatedly. In the end, when he lets go of his "doubts and thoughts," he finds Him pervading all and himself nowhere (v. 58). He purifies his mind by renouncing greed, pride, and attachment. He engages in spiritual practice with focused attention to loosen the hold of his lower self. He offers "hundreds of prayers" in the daytime and maintains his vigil during the night to come closer to God.

Without an oar,
　　I ferried the boat across.
I killed pride, greed, and attachment.

With devotion, I searched for the Lord—
only then I recognized my higher Self. (v. 23)

Through constant practice, he sacrifices "the poison of [his] animal nature" and he controls his ego. He seeks solitude in the backwoods, away from the hustle and bustle of life, and he firmly settles in a cave. He experiences the cave as a grave for his material aspirations. Here, he puts "to sleep" his desire for material things forever as he purifies his body by engaging in austerities. In a verse, Nūruddīn says:

Living in backwoods,
I made my body
tremble in fear.
First, I made a cave—
After removing inner impurities,
I made Him reveal Himself.
I turned the cave into my grave.
With saffron and camphor[40]
I purified my body.
My desire for good things
I put to sleep in the cave. (v. 14)

In the solitude of the cave, he remembers God day and night and becomes absorbed in meditation. He sees himself turning from "ashes into gold." The sacred words purify his inner self. He goes through various stages of purification, which are symbolized in the above verse by "saffron" and "camphor." He feels the proximity of divine presence and finds "peace near Him." He realizes that he had wrongly "looked for Him in the outer world" when He was in the inner world. As he totally surrenders himself to the divine will, he is filled with bliss.

---

[40] "saffron" and "camphor" symbolize stages of purification on the Sufi path.

After spending many years in the cave performing austerities, Nūruddīn reached a very advanced state spiritually. He attracted many disciples, who gathered around him and sought his guidance. He eventually left the cave and travelled to different parts of Kashmir to spread his message. Many villages around Kashmir "connect at least a spring, a chinar tree or an elevated place with his memory. Many caves are revered as places where he meditated."[41]

As the Rishī movement expanded, Nūruddīn moved to Tsrar,[42] a dense forest, which was soon inhabited and eventually turned into the main center of the Rishī Sufi order and it is here that he died in 1439. Tsrar Sharif, where Nūruddīn's tomb is located, is a pilgrimage place for both Muslims and Non-Muslims alike. The purity and simplicity of Nūruddīn's life and his status as a patron saint of Kashmir is attested by the fact that the Afghan Governor Ata Muhammad Khan in the early nineteenth century took the public sentiment into account as he struck coins in his name.[43] In more recent time, to promote the stewardship of Kashmiri forests, the state forest department has adopted a verse saying of Nūruddīn, "ann poshi tele yeli van poshi" (if the forest flourishes, the food is plentiful).[44]

Metaphysical Thought

Nūruddīn Rishi's verses are permeated with the concept of the Unity of God, and he presents this idea in a variety of ways. In a verse, he says: "The first letter 'alif' represents one God. He permeates all from the first to the last" (v. 46). In another verse, the Oneness of God is presented in the form of the first cause that comes before the manifestation.

---

[41] Gauhar, p. 72.

[42] Tsrar Sharif is located 32 kilometers south-west of Srinagar, Kashmir.

[43] Sufi, *Kashir*, vol. I, p. 101.

[44] Gauhar, p. 72.

God is thus the source of light that illuminates the universe and brings it forth into existence.

He who is here is also there.
He is omnipresent.
He is the soldier and
He is the chariot.
Himself hidden—
He is omnipotent. (v. 40)

Even as He is the creator of the universe, He is beyond it, or in other words He transcends it and hence, is always veiled. Yet, as the creator of the cosmos, He is one with the cosmos, which manifests His attributes as seen in the infinite multiplicity of things. Nūruddīn says: "He Himself plays the reality of the totality without a moment of interruption" and "He is everywhere—you are nowhere" (v. 45). The line "He Himself plays the reality of the totality" does not mean that God (i.e. Allah) becomes identical with His creation, because, according to Muslim belief, Existence only belongs to God. Thus there are two aspects of the Ultimate Reality—one is reflected in God's transcendence and another aspect is God's immanence. As transcendence or as Essence (*dhāt*), God is unknowable and inaccessible. However, as immanence, something of the divine attributes can be known through the existent objects of the world, as everything that exists in the cosmos lies in the Reality of One God. A Koranic verse says, "God encompasses all things in knowledge" (65:12). To explain this idea, Nūruddīn uses the analogy of water in different forms—ice, icicles, and snow—all these forms are transformed into the same water once "the sun rises in the east, [and] the three are turned into one" (v. 50). Similarly, things in the cosmos appear in a variety of forms and shapes, but eventually all individual forms in the manifest cosmos dissolve into their non-existent status in the all-encompassing knowledge of God.

The Ultimate Reality or God is a mystery, which is

incomprehensible and indescribable. Sufis use the analogy of the white light passing through a prism and breaking into different colors as an example to show how the invisible light contains different colors of the spectrum and yet in itself transcends all colors. Or another analogy used is that of the white light passing through a colored glass and taking on the color of the glass. Similarly, when the divine light (*nūr*) falls on things, they come into existence and manifest their own immutable attributes. Though it is impossible to know God in Himself, we can, however, find out something about Him through His manifest attributes reflected in the things of the cosmos, which are signs pointing towards God. To put it another way, the manifest cosmos is unreal since it does not truly exist. However, it can be said that the manifest cosmos reflects the attributes of God, Who exists. A Koranic verse says, "Wheresoever you turn, there is the Face of God" (2:115). Every created thing manifests one or more qualities of God and hence, in coming into being, it glorifies the Lord, without Whom it would not exist. In a verse, Nūruddīn says:

God is One—
  His names are many.
Not a blade of grass exists
  without remembering Him.
Consider life a fortnight.
Not even a fly exists
  without His sustenance. (v. 39)

All created things remember Him to the extent their existence allows it, because they would not exist without divine sustenance. Even a blade of grass or a small creature, like a fly, remembers Him because He brought them forth into existence. The created universe is in time and hence, subject to continuous change and fluctuation, whereas God in Himself is eternal and everlasting.

Nūruddīn Rishi's concept of the Unity of God or the Unity

of Being as reflected in his verses can be compared to the concept of *wahdat al-wujūd* present in the works of the great 12th century mystic philosopher Ibn al-'Arabī. It is important to elaborate on this notion to get a deeper understanding of Nūruddīn's metaphysics and how it is linked to his moral and ecological vision. One has to remember that Nūruddīn lived in the countryside and his teachings were based on experience rather than on any study of Sufi texts. His knowledge of the Unity of God is that of a mystic, who through visionary experiences learns something about God in his similarity as manifested through His creation. In contrast to this divine unveiling, the knowledge of God shown by religious scholars is based on intellectual theorization, as they spend considerable effort in defining God in how He is different and totally inaccessible to His creation.

Ibn al-'Arabī defines the word *wujūd* in its highest sense as the Essence of God or *dhāt al haqīqā,* which is unknowable and inaccessible. The manifest things are eternally present as non-existent immutable essences in the infinite knowledge of God. Out of mercy God creates the cosmos because the non-existent essences are longing to become manifest to enjoy their attributes in their fullness. It is through shining the light of *wujūd* on the immutable entities present in His knowledge that the cosmos is created. Ibn al-'Arabī refers to the Koranic verses, which describe the creation of the cosmos when the All Merciful God exhaled and in the Breath words were spoken to make immutable essences come into existence. Thus, the words cannot be seen apart from God's Breath and creatures not apart from the words that called them out. Even though God's Breath can exist without the words, the words cannot exist without the Breath, because it is the latter which gave creatures existence. In one sense, the universe is other than God, but, in another sense, it is a part of God since its existence is permeated with the *wujūd* or the Real or *al Haqq*. The words spoken by God are the same as the Breath and the Breath is the same as the All Merciful. Thus, the cosmos is both He and not He. Things in the cosmos are identical with the Real and different from the Real at the same time. In order to explain this idea further, Ibn al-'Arabī uses the example of an image reflected in a polished mirror. The image in the mirror is neither identical to the object reflected nor to the mirror which reflects it. It is both "is" and "is not." Thus, the things in the universe are both He and not He because it is impossible to know Him in his Essence, but something about Him can be known through the attributes manifested in the cosmos through the power of His *wujūd,* which is One Reality. Similarly, what is seen in imagination in the form of visionary mystic experiences is both He and not He, as it is impossible to know Him in Himself. The removal of each veil reveals yet another veil. It is through the veils God shows that He cannot be identified with any specific image or idea. God, as the Real or *al Haqq,* is beyond all phenomenal characterization, whether in the material or imaginal reality.[45]

Another aspect of Ibn al-'Arabī's thought that is of relevance to understand Nūruddīn Rishī's moral vision relates to his doctrine of perfect man (*al-insān al-kāmil*). A Koranic verse says that "God taught Adam all names" (2:31), which has been interpreted to mean that human beings have the potential to actualize all names of God to achieve perfection. The name "Allah" is an all comprehensive name for God, which includes all other names. The Koran and the Hadith note ninety nine Most Beautiful Names of God, for example, Alive, Powerful, Knowing, Desiring, Merciful, Speaking, and Generous, among others. Thus, "the divine names allow us to understand many realities of obvious

---

[45] Ibn al-'Arabī, *Futūhāt al-Makkiyya,* trans. W. Chittick, in *The Sufi Path of Knowledge* and his more detailed translation of selections from *Futūhāt al-Makkiyya* in *The Self Disclosure of God: Principles of Ibn al-'Arabī's Cosmology.*

diversity (*ikhtilāf*). The names are attributed only to God, for He is the object named by them, but He does not become multiple (*takaththur*) through them."[46] The loci of manifestation of names are thus plural or the effects are plural, but their reference is to the Unity of Being. Later scholars have labeled the Most Beautiful Names as the universal names of God, whereas all other names of things in the manifest cosmos are called His particular names. Human beings, because of their latent potential to actualize all divine names, can in fact transform themselves over the course of their lifetime and turn into a saint from an ignorant fool. The traits of knowledge, speech, generosity, justice, compassion, love, patience, and so on might reveal themselves as one or more fully manifested traits in noble human beings who aspire to the highest. When all divine traits are in full manifestation, there is an overflow of nobility and goodness. For most humans, however, this state is only an ideal state to be approached, but not to be fully realized.[47]

While humans represent the undifferentiated Unity of names or attributes as the microcosm, the cosmos, as the macrocosm, is the differentiated manifestation of God's attributes and each reflects the other. Ibn al-'Arabī even calls humans the spirit of cosmos, as they have the ability to shape the cosmos, but the cosmos is passive and unconscious and hence, cannot act on humans. The more a society is composed of human beings aspiring toward noble, divine traits, the greater the chance of the cosmos and things in the cosmos evolving into a better state. The noble, divine traits can thus be seen as ethical values to create a just society. The unmanifest form of God is inaccessible and unknowable, but the manifest form can reach full disclosure in perfect human beings, who thus represent the full potential of the

46 Ibid, *Futūhāt al-Makkiyya*, trans. W. Chittick, in *The Ṣufi Path of Knowledge*, p. 35.
47 Ibid, pp. 274–78.

nobility of the being. For Ibn al-'Arabī, the goal of religion is to create a society with perfect human beings, who have actualized most or all of God's noble traits or attributes. He writes that the full disclosure of divine attributes only takes place in prophets and messengers and, to a smaller degree, in saints *(Auwliyā)*. The saints might show the full disclosure of one or several of the traits, but not all the traits.[48]

Nūruddīn Rishī was not a philosopher, but his poetic corpus is based on the experience about which Ibn 'al-Arabī theorizes in his extensive works. So we can make use of Ibn 'al-Arabī's philosophy as a heuristic device to better understand Nūruddīn's worldview and how it manifested in his lifestyle and his teachings. Nūruddīn emphsizes in all his verses the need to engage in good deeds in order to approach closer to God. However, those who engage in good deeds must first work on their character so they are drawn to good acts that produce good results for them as well as for others. In the context of Nūruddīn's poetic corpus, the accumulation of good deeds thus means to build one's character through renouncing base traits like pride, anger, hate, jealousy, and greed, and assuming noble traits like compassion, love, purity, and generosity. Such a transformation becomes the foundation for engaging in selfless acts. All traits originate in God, in Whom they are present in the truest form. Humans can, however, aspire to some degree of perfection by cultivating these traits as they relate to the world. Such a belief is intimately linked to the idea that the created world is not our 'other' as the same divine consciousness or God's *wujūd* (existence/being) or *nūr* (light) permeates the humans and the non-humans in the cosmos with varying degrees of intensity. The source of multiplicity and difference is God, who can exist without

[48] Chittick, "Ethics and Antinomianism" and "Ṣelf Ḳnowledge and Original Disposition" in *Imaginal Worlds: Ibn al-'Arabī and the Problem of Religious Diversity*, pp. 39–64.

the created universe and the creatures that inhabit it, but the created universe cannot exist without Him.

In his verses, Nūruddīn repeatedly says that the way to get closer to God is by renouncing human traits and opening up to divine traits in order to move closer to the divine realities represented by the names. All entities in the cosmos share in God's attributes, as they come into being through God's light. However, not all entities can manifest all names or attributes equally. In a verse, Nūruddīn says:

— He adorns every attribute.
No birth or death for the Essence.
A superior place is
  bestowed on humans.
If you are wise,
  you will meditate on the Self. (v. 45)

According to the Sufi thought, there is a hierarchy in the cosmos; for example, stones are different from plants, which in their turn are different from animals, even as they all share the same light to varying levels of intensity. Stones are passive and lack the attributes of knowing or desiring, but as we go up the hierarchy, life acquires more intensity and more attributes are reflected in the entities. Humans thus occupy the highest place in the visible cosmos as Adam was created in the image of God. Even though humans possess all divine traits in latent form, they do not manifest all the traits or manifest them with the same intensity. The human effort towards perfection is always a work in progress.

Nūruddīn says that a person to whom the divine knowledge is revealed, he continuously remembers God. He renounces love for the body and the ego and believes he is nobody and he has no name. The focus here is not on adopting divine attributes: it is rather on renouncing human traits, which opens the individual to the divine attributes. Thus, he says:

Remove the rust from
your heart as if from a mirror.
That is how you will be
acquainted with Him.
So youthful is your face and body.
Die before your death—
that is knowledge. (v. 64)

To the extent that the traveler on the path diminishes his own egocentric self, the base human traits associated with him also diminish in intensity. He thus opens the way for the manifestation of divine traits as he approaches closer to God. The aim of spiritual practice is to eventually experience the non-existence of one's own essence, as the state of existence is a borrowed affair from God. This idea is expressed in the following verse:

If you realize the One,
the self will disappear.
So much brilliance emanates from the One.
Intellect and anxiety have no place there.
Who could drink from that river, my dear? (v. 42)

In Nūruddīn's verses, the lower self or the ego is linked to the physical body and its desire for material possessions and pleasures. In a verse that reflects the Koranic verses (15:28–29; 32:7–9; 38:71–72), Nūruddīn says: "[God] created man with the earthly nature and shaped him in the frame of clay. He created all natural things from clay" (v. 48). Then, he breathed the divine spirit into him. The spirit thus possesses all the angelic attributes of luminosity, subtlety, and unity, whereas the body, made out of clay, is marked by denseness, darkness, and dispersion. These two different modalities, the spirit and the body, are brought into interaction through the soul, which thus combines in it the unity and dispersion, subtlety and denseness, and luminosity and darkness. Humans are a mix of two qualities, one pushing them towards the material reality of density and darkness, and the other towards the spiritual reality of luminosity and subtlety. The soul (*nafs*) or the individual awareness as the intermediary between the body and the spirit shares the world of light reflected by the spirit (*rūh*) as it desires, knows, and illuminates, but it is also connected to the world of ignorance, darkness, and the lack of divinity as reflected in the body.

Within the above broader context of the reality of the soul and the spirit, Nūruddīn comments on the finer connections between the mind, the body, and the ego. At birth, the mind and the body start working together and as both grow and mature, they mutually affect one another. The mind that shapes the ego and the body that is the medium through which the body-mind complex functions in the workings of the ego are important in their own way.

After birth, the body
  joined with "I" becomes precious.
He who controls the body,
  his impurities are removed.
In the end, it becomes auspicious.
He who controls the mind purifies his nature.
For him, the door to the inner sanctuary is open. (v. 89)

Thus, both the mind and the body need to be purified in order to discipline the lower self. In the end, the very organs, the body and the mind, that pull the individual into ignorance and darkness, can become sanctified and a site of divine disclosure and a vehicle for the actualization of divine names.

Nūruddīn contrasts the above-mentioned inner purification with the external purification, which might satisfy an individual's desire for cleanliness, but will not help him move forward on the path. If external cleanliness through bathing were enough, then "the nature of the fish and the crocodile would be the same," as both have their permanent abode in water (v. 126). In another verse, he says, scrubbing the body with soap and water will not make someone clean in the spiritual sense. Nor will carrying a rosary and a staff and wearing tattered garments turn somebody into a holy person. Acting as a holy person is thus different from actually being a holy person. So a serious seeker becomes holy or pure within first, as without purity of one's thoughts, noble or selfless actions are impossible. Thus, he says:

Don't rub your body—
  the soap will not clean it.
The rosary, staff and the patched robe—
  these tricks will not lead you to Him.
Renounce desires, my dear,
  and become a servant.

——

The same Lord is both here and there.
Supplicate and seek refuge.
Walk on the right path
  and not on the crooked one.
He who purifies five sense organs,
  sees in the heart and is ecstatic. (v. 122)

The best way to find Him is thus to "renounce desires and become a servant," which means to submit one's ego to the divine will. Also, it is important to purify one's senses so one's attention is always directed inwards. Nūruddīn constantly reminds people to give up their preoccupation with the pleasures and comforts of the world. Instead of giving in to desires, he advises them to practice detachment in their thoughts and actions. The detachment must be accompanied by inner purification, which means that seekers must give up all base traits in their relationship to the world, for example, greed, hate, anger, and attachment, among others. Performing good deeds selflessly is another way to loosen the grasp of the lower self.

Remember God and practice austerities.
When your appetite for food is lost,
  you will become graceful.
Your greed and anger will die
  and hate and pride will not last.
Performing actions with detachment will bear fruit.
Only then empty vessels will be filled to the brim. (v. 91)

Cultivating purity with respect to thoughts and actions is thus necessary to proceed on the path, as only then the "empty vessels" of individual awareness will be filled with spiritual awareness. Sufis describe the heart as the organ of vision and compare it to a mirror, which needs to be continuously polished through remembering God. In the above verse, the reference is to the purification of one's senses, thoughts, and actions, which thus prepares the heart for divine unveiling.

According to Nūruddīn, human existence unfolds as the soul grows and discovers its true nature and becomes aware of the contradictions of its own nature and the two paths open to it, one leading upwards to the lightness, luminosity, and subtlety of the spirit and the other downwards to the denseness and darkness of matter. It is in this context that the role of guidance and misguidance is brought into play. Those who are guided by a genuine teacher achieve felicity and those who are misguided stray from the path. The greatest obstacle on the spiritual path is the undisciplined and out-of-control lower self that pulls the individual downwards to darkness and density, away from light and knowledge of God. Nūruddīn compares the lower self to a thief and as such, it corrupts the higher aspirations of an individual. If it is not brought under control, it will keep asking for more to fulfill its desires. The ego, constantly on the lookout for gratifying its desires, must be tamed if the seeker wants to proceed forward on the path. However, one cannot simply renounce the lower self and move forward on the path. A "bargain has to be struck with the lower self," which means it has to be disciplined and its nature recognized.

Nūruddīn emphasizes in his verses that the first step for the traveler on the path is to withdraw one's attention from the outside world and engage in inner contemplation. He compares the five sense organs to five rivers, which continuously take in impressions from the outer world through sight, smell, touch, sound, and taste. If one withdraws attention from the external reality, the stream of the outside world flowing in is brought to a standstill.

Control the flow of the five rivers—
  breathe in deeply.
Use the same breath to control your pride.
It will lead to valuable knowledge. (v. 117)

Achieving focused attention is facilitated by meditating on the breath, which is a basic meditation in Sufism. It is usually accompanied by reciting the name Allah or one of Allah's names. So calming the mind through the control of breathing and through constant recitation of divine names is an important aspect of the spiritual journey. An inattentive mind is the basis of an undisciplined ego that is the source of desires and hence, an obstacle on one's journey to come closer to God. Nūruddīn says:

One moment I inhaled
  and another moment I exhaled.
My attachment disappeared instantly.
In a moment one step became a mile.
My [ego]-tiger became weak instantly. (v. 12)

Nūruddīn compares the Sufi path to different steps involved in cultivating the land to grow a crop—a metaphor to which the people in the countryside could relate. Cultivation is a lengthy process that involves sowing seeds, watering and weeding, nurturing, and finally harvesting the crop when the farmer takes on the role of a trader as he gathers the fruit of his labor and exchanges it for monetary value. Nūruddīn impresses on the country folk in a simple language that they must lead a disciplined life in order to overcome their lower self. Thus, he says: "One who sows seeds, endures the weeding process. Searchingly, he pulls out weeds and old branches. One who sows in spring, weighs in autumn. He enters heaven as a trader" (v. 60). For a seeker to become a trader in the spiritual sense requires sowing the seeds of good attributes or cultivating good traits through remembering the divine names until they permeate the being and transform the character. This process must be accompanied by continuous attention towards disciplining the mind and the body, comparable to the weeding process in planting a crop. Just as the weeds are pulled out to have a good crop, similarly bad thoughts need to be renounced through remembering God and performing austerities. Thus, Nūruddīn says:

— Heart is a fish: don't leave it dry.
Irrigate it with the remembrance of God:
 it will flourish then.
The self is a jewel: don't lose it.
Lord is the Beloved:
 He will thus be pleased. (v. 29)

Through remembering God, the seeker focuses on the life-giving traits to illuminate the consciousness. The preoccupation with material reality is equivalent to associating with ignorance and darkness as true existence only belongs to God. Offering prayers regularly with sincerity opens up the heart, purifies the soul, and transforms one's thoughts and actions. The negative thoughts are thus eliminated and the focus shifted to the positive thoughts. Only then do the seeds blossom into noble traits that manifest as compassion, love, caring, and selflessness, among others.

Nūruddīn's teachings are couched in a moral framework

rooted in the Islamic tradition. He urges people to lead responsible lives so they create a better world for themselves and for their community. He warns people if they continue to engage in bad deeds due to their ego-centric attitude, they will suffer on their death, as they will fall into the fire, unable to cross the bridge of Ṣirāṭ.[49] Those who have accumulated good deeds, on the other hand, will remain unscathed by the fire and go to heaven. Thus, he says:

> Those who engage in spiritual discipline
> and who offer prayers
> are truly born to this world.
> They plant in abundance and nurture it.
> On ripening, they have a big harvest.
> They will go across and
> emerge from the fire.
> God Himself will reward them for it. (v. 61)

According to Nūruddīn, people who engage in austerities are truly born to the world, as their life is aligned with the spiritual reality. Such people have experienced their spiritual birth, which shapes their thoughts and actions. They engage in good deeds and are rewarded for that in the next world as the fire of hell loses its power on them. Such people are not afraid of death. In fact, to them "the grave is like a bed of flowers." However, people, "who do not remember God and the Prophet, they are born to the world as body," (v. 105) and hence, they experience the death of the physical body as their final end, which fills them with extreme fear. For such people, "the grave is a dark abyss." In yet another verse, Nūruddīn tells people that they should "die while alive," which means they should kill their desire for worldly things.

[49] According to Muslim belief, all must cross the bridge of Ṣirāṭ after death to go to paradise. The narrow, razor-thin bridge covers the raging fire of hell. The sinners are unable to cross it and fall into the fire, while the good people go across the bridge to paradise.

When they do so, they ascend to the higher states of consciousness and their awareness of the spiritual reality expands. As a result, their sense of ego increasingly diminishes. In a verse, he says:

In whom the knowledge dawns, he knows—
He devotedly remembers God.
He who kills pride and renounces the ego [says]—
"I am nobody and I have no name."
He who experiences Him,
  his duality fades away. (v. 41)

Travelers on the path, Nūruddīn says, are thus transformed from somebody with a name to nobody with no name. In such a state, they surrender themselves totally to the divine will that works through them. They thus become perfect disclosures of God, as they completely obliterate their own existence and subsist in God. This level of perfection, of course, is only for spiritually advanced people or saints, but common people can at least aspire to this ideal state.

The realization of the Oneness of God in Nūruddīn's thought is thus closely linked to purifying oneself of egoistical traits and going beyond the intellectual understanding of the divine reality. In his verses, the relationship between man and God is not that of identity. He notes that humans are blessed with special grace in that they have been fashioned in the image of God and hence, have potential to actualize all divine attributes. In order to do so, however, they must turn within, purify themselves of negative traits, and aspire to come closer to God. He describes God as a Friend. The relationship is that of proximity rather than identity.

Alone am I—
I yearn to be with my Friend.
Every moment I want to be with Him.
Without my Friend,

flowers will turn into thorns.
Wherever my Friend is,
there is my Mecca. (v. 25)

Like other Sufis, Nūruddīn describes God as the Beloved and it is through love that humans can come closer to God. The fate of the lover is the annihilation of the self in order to experience the divine reality. Thus, "A lover burns with love—He shines like gold. He whose heart is afflicted with love—he is the one who will be joined with the higher Self" (v. 37). In another verse, he says:

Whoever starts a vigil at His door,
He offers him His own
nectar to drink.
A variety of plays—
Only one is the Director.
Whom He loves,
he is the one who attains. (v. 26)

He compares here seekers to characters in different plays. As such they forge different relationships with their Lord, the personalized form of the Divine, and as a result, they have different types of experiences. But all these multiple dramas in the world are directed by one Director and that is God. Since it is impossible for the creatures to relate to God in His all comprehensive role, Nūruddīn depicts the relationship between the two as that of a Lord and His vassal. God's love for the servant is as important as the servant's love for the Lord. Thus, renouncing the human traits is indispensable to open up to the divine attributes, which would bring the seeker closer to God. This perhaps explains the Rishī Sufis' extreme austerities and penance to come closer to human perfection, in so far as one's human existence can allow that to happen. In a verse, Nūruddīn says:

After killing the lower self,
  those who become disciplined,
    they suffer and act as servants.
Searching for God truthfully,
  they consider everything as ashes. (v. 36)

Nūruddīn vigorously critiques religious scholars, who accumulate knowledge and then dispense advice, but never practice what they preach. He describes them as sellers of goods as they are more interested in accumulating money and fame rather than having spiritual experience. They read and write a lot, but their attachment to this world does not end. Such people, he says, are filled with pride and arrogance and they are always engaged in competition with one another. Their book-based knowledge gives them an intellectual understanding of God, who is beyond intellectual categories. Thus, they lack the power of direct experience, which is a mystic's source of divine knowledge. Since religious scholars base their descriptions of God on rational thought rather than on direct divine unveiling, they can only talk in terms of incomparability between the Creator and creatures, as nothing in the cosmos can be used to talk about God in his Essence. They make no attempt to know God in his similarity through cultivating an attitude of love for the differentiated multiplicity of the cosmos. For that reason, they do not grasp the divinity in multiplicity, as experienced by mystics. As they lack direct experience, they show off their intellectual prowess and their facility with words to impress the common folk as they dispense advice. Thus, he says:

A learned man churns nectar.
A stream of drops trickles down his face.
A pile of books he has in front of him—
  Consulting these, he acts passionate.
When we begin to see, he is empty inside.
He forgets himself while reproaching others. (v. 76)

In yet another verse, Nūruddīn focuses on the intellectual knowledge of religious scholars as "first they read, and then they preach." They are honored by the common people, who believe that "goodness lies in listening" to the preachers' words that would lead them to accumulate good deeds. For scholars, however, preaching is an occupation to better their material situation in life. Thus, Nūruddīn says: "They build houses that reach the sky as if the world is a heap of ashes. Ignoring the hereafter, they care only for wealth" (v. 78). Mystics do not use books to preach, as their knowledge of God is based on direct experience. Through their devotion and love for God, they have some knowledge of Him in similarity, and they embody this perspective in their teaching. In knowing Him through similarity, it is not rational analysis, but imagination that allows mystics to get some insight into the divine reality.

Sufis in general describe the cosmos as consisting of three dimensions, the spiritual, the imaginal, and the corporeal reality and behind these three dimensions is the foundational consciousness of God as Essence. The material reality or the physical body of the human dimension is connected to the spiritual reality through the interface of imagination. The faculty of imagination lies in the middle zone between the manifest and the unmanifest or the seen and the unseen world. The imaginal reality is the *barzakh* or isthmus between the corporeal and spiritual realities. As a *barzakh*, it possesses the attributes of light, creativity, life, and knowledge of the divine Spirit as well as darkness, ignorance, and non-existence of the corporeal reality.[50] It is to express this aspect of mystical experience that Nūruddīn says: "Those who dissolve in the sacred vision within, act deaf and dumb on the outside. Unscathed they emerge from the fire— Priceless jewels thus they are" (v. 53). The divine unveiling

[50] Ibn al-'Arabī, *Futūhāt al-Makkiyya*, trans. William Chittick, in *The Sufi Path of Knowledge*, pp. 112–143.

gives mystics a deeper understanding of the need to develop humility and love in one's relationship to created things, all of which spring forth from the same source. The mystical experience is based on inner revelation in the imaginal realm that brings together the seen and the unseen world. Thus, he says: "whose soul receives the revelation within, purged is he of the shivers of hell" and he "enters the company of the Lord" (v. 143). As a mystic of the highest caliber, Nūruddīn's experience of God is based on divine unveiling rather than intellectual knowledge gathered from reading books, and his whole world view and teaching are guided by this unveiling.

Ethical and Ecological Vision

Nūruddīn's philosophical vision is not an abstract representation of reality to be comprehended intellectually. It is a practical philosophy. He lived what he preached to his community. He taught people that social forces have an impact on people's life and thus could create conditions that are not suitable for the unfolding of the inner life. In a verse, Nūruddīn embodies such forces in the image of the tiger and the jackal:

> As tigers retreat into caves,
> jackals howl.
> As the big house crumbles,
> the little houses are illuminated.
> As the poor flock together,
> kings are troubled.
> As the sheep sit in the open, cooks suffer. (v. 132)

The smaller animals, the jackals, come out of hiding and express their nature fully in the absence of a predator like the tiger. Or again, when a big house crumbles, the little houses start getting light. Thus, what is suppressed or hidden from sight can express itself fully if the blocking agent is removed. Similarly, if the poor flock together, the dynamics of the society changes and those in power are troubled and hence, they might engage in actions to prevent such a change. Or again, if the sheep were not killed and could freely roam around, the cooks will feel deprived of cooking fancy dishes. The purpose of these suggestive comparisons is to make people realize that there are indeed social and physical barriers in society and these barriers need to be recognized and overcome in order to make progress.

An interesting legend recounts how once Nūruddīn was invited to a feast as an honored guest, but he was not allowed into the home by the servants, who did not recognize him as he was dressed in a patched robe. When the hosts did not see him at the appointed time, they sent someone to fetch him. This time he was dressed in a long sleeved formal robe. He was given an honored seat amongst the guests. As the feast was served, Nūruddīn unrolled the sleeves of his robe and dipped them in the dishes served on his plate. When asked, why he was acting so strangely, he responded: "The feast was not really for Nūruddīn but for the long sleeves."[51] This incident was meant to teach the guests that one's preoccupation with external appearances could be misleading in assessing the worth of what they come across.

In addition to commenting upon the societal impact on the individual, in some verses Nūruddīn reflects on the individual's responsibilities to take control of one's spiritual practice. He says, each individual has the responsibility to make use of opportunities he or she is given in order to bring them to fruition. A dead flower cannot ask for anything from its own existence or from the garden because it has already lost that opportunity.

A flower whose dear life is destroyed
can ask for nothing from
the flower or the garden.

[51] Sufi, *Kashir*, vol. I, p. 101.

He who falls asleep in a secluded place
can ask for nothing from
the bright light of the sun. (v. 86)

Similarly, if a traveler on the path is in an ideal situation to make progress on his journey, he could miss the opportunity through inaction, suggestively communicated in the above verse as a person falling asleep in a secluded place and thus missing the opportunity to appreciate the bright light of the sun and to seek the sun within. Then, there are people, who are unable to make use of an opportunity due to their physical or psychological limitations that prevent them from utilizing it to explore the higher dimensions of reality. He uses the following analogies to explain this idea to his listeners:

A toothless man cannot break a walnut.
A cripple has no use for a bow and arrow.
A pearl necklace is of no use to a dog.
A blind man appreciates not a beautiful woman. (v. 131)

The individual short-comings could prevent a person from recognizing or utilizing an opportunity for advancing on the path. However, people are sometime blessed with qualities that take them straight to their goal, even as others might be physically or psychologically unequipped for it. Thus, he says: "An eagle knows how to go after the prey," but a "barren woman knows not how to deliver a baby," because she has not experienced it herself (v. 133). The point he makes in these verses is that the world is full of differences and individuals are unique in the way they respond to their existential situation based on their innate qualities and the external circumstances that determine their life experiences.

In many verses, Nūruddīn dwells on the contradictions of the world, as it is filled with truth seekers and pleasure seekers, gullible ones and those who are divinely inspired and those who spend "their life in despair." We see at "the door of the ignorant, the wise are turned away," as the ignorant do not know the value of wisdom. Also, the ignorant ones get fed, whereas the wise ones are hungry, the "good toil and the wicked devour," or "the devout are bewildered and the ignorant happy" (v. 118).

Nūruddīn uses the example of the marsh grass to explain to his listeners that the societal perception of who or what is inferior or superior is not cast in stone. It is possible to transcend such labels if one has the strength and persistence to achieve one's goal. The marsh grass is considered inferior and not good enough to be used even for animal fodder. But its stem has a special quality, which lies in its sturdiness and strength for binding things together. Even though the general opinion is that the marsh flower is of inferior quality, due to the sturdiness and strength of its stem, it becomes a part of the wreath that adorns a king's forehead.

Of inferior variety is
  the stem of the marsh flower—
    the horse and the cattle don't eat it.
In a wreath when it reaches the king's head,
  no longer is it seen as inferior. (v. 93)

Nūruddīn uses the above verse to point out that people might think they are inferior because of their birth or their station, but if they have inner strength and perseverance, they can transcend the social labels or the accident of their birth and achieve unimaginable heights, which would result in others revising their earlier views.

In many verses, Nūruddīn comments on the qualities people should cultivate in order to contribute to their own and their community's well-being. In a long poem, he lists the attributes of a person who should be called a Muslim. He is the one who fights wicked deeds, possesses humility, and follows what he preaches to others. Such a person's body is "fragrant" and his "face is awake" and he is "without anger." A Muslim, he says, "renounces anger, greed, and pride" and brings his undisciplined ego under control. He "shares his meal with others," "fasts on holy days," seeks out the company of good people and renounces that of bad people. Such a man purifies his mind and engages day and night in remembering God as he "takes himself and others across the ocean." Thus, the divine attributes of selflessness, purity, nonattachment, compassion, humility, and generosity are embodied in Nūruddīn's definition of a true Muslim.

In the above context, he says, if Non-Muslims engaged in good deeds from a young age, it will help them on any path. Observing austerities will open God's door and their attachment will disappear by itself. They must, however, purify their thoughts and actions and remember God with single-minded devotion. Nūruddīn affirmed religious difference and emphasized the need to cultivate good moral values. He aspired for a just society where different members lived together harmoniously, irrespective of their caste, class, or religious affiliation. In a verse, he says: "Born from a single Father and Mother—Do not discriminate between Muslims and Hindus" (v. 139).

Nūruddīn was also against the caste system prevalent in medieval Kashmir that divided the Hindu society into different segments. He reminds people that all people are created equal so they should develop love for the other by perfecting their love of God. He thus promotes love and compassion and advises people to help others in the community and share what they have with them. All humans, he says, have descended from a single father and mother and all are children of the same God, so we should not differentiate between people on the basis of religion, caste, or creed. Thus, he says:

Adam was the father—
Mother Eve followed him.
Where did lower castes come from? (v. 135)

Nūruddīn's verses not only emphasize compassion for fellow beings, but also towards animals. He subsisted on a vegetarian diet all his life because he believed killing animals was cruel. In a verse, he vividly describes the cruel treatment of animals used for farming purposes and when they are not fit to plough the land, they are subject to other atrocities to get as much service from them as possible. And when no longer of any use, they are killed. He says:

A buffalo is raised on fodder.
In spring, he is tied to a plough.
If he sits, they burn a packed sheaf of grass under him.
After saying "hui," they raise and twist his tail.
If he can't walk, he is put to use in the miller's shop.
Covering his eyes, his world is made dark.
In the end, his skin is removed with a sharp knife.
If you are attached to the body, the world is tainted. (v. 73)

Humans thus heedlessly and heartlessly act toward other creatures, who, they believe, were created specifically for their use. According to Nūruddīn, people should recognize that the same divine reality permeates both the human and the nonhuman world. They would then develop reverence for the non-human world and be more compassionate and considerate toward others. In a verse, he says:

It is not good to slaughter a sheep.
Recognize that only He apportions.
If you follow my teaching—
  only One Spirit plays in the big world. (v. 74)

Nūruddīn's compassion extended not only to animals, but also to plants, trees, and green vegetation around him. In a set of verses that have been preserved in a dialogue form, he addresses some women whom he comes across on one of his journeys. As he sees them cutting the grass with a sickle, he tells them that they are destroying "the fragrance of grass." They are also killing countless little creatures as they cut the grass. People had dreamed of this "spring greenery in the winter," so why destroy it, he asks. He urges the women to be heedful of their act and think of it in the broader context of the results of their action.

> Without good deeds, no goodness is within.
> You are destroying the fragrance of grass.
> We dreamed of the spring greenery in the winter.
> Reverence can be found only in the city outskirts.
> After killing so many, what would be your reckoning?
> Learn to remove your inborn instincts. (v. 70)

In another verse, Nūruddīn says that "on witnessing such sights, Rishīs retreated to backwoods [and] they abstained from delicious food so nature is not made dreary." He tells them, it is wrong to destroy something that has life and urges them not to "sacrifice life for nothing" (vv. 71, 72). He regards it as a purely human trait to heedlessly think only of one's own survival, without paying any attention to how one's actions might affect others. It is for this reason that he asks them to renounce the "inborn human instinct" to consider all non-human life for human use and exploitation. One of the women, Shyam Māji, replies that she is cutting the grass to bring it home to feed her cow, who gives her milk. And she enjoys milk, ghee, and whey and the hungry ones at home need to be fed.[52] Nuruddīn responds by saying that grass has life and life should never be taken for nothing. But he also admits that sometimes such actions cannot be avoided. He tells Shyam Māji the reason he asked her the question was to find out her motivation to cut the grass. Nūruddīn's exchange with the woman shows that he was against any unnecessary destruction of nature and wanted people to develop an awareness of the precious nature of all life around them.

---

[52] Parimoo, pp. 271–76.

As Nūruddīn travelled throughout Kashmir, he taught people how to live a more spiritual and moral life. He wanted them to cultivate ecological and ethical awareness as manifested in the daily act of living. His verses emphasized that both animals and plants are filled with life and hence, not to be dominated or exploited. In a verse, he says:

Why do you kill fish
  to appease the self?
Those who kill living creatures
  to feed the living are
    the deluded of the world. (v. 75)

Nūruddīn casts the killing of living creatures in the broader framework of the consequences of bad deeds as he promotes the sanctity of all life. Those who destroy life, he says, will have to answer in the hereafter when Nakir and Munkir, the two angels at the graveside of those who die, according to Muslim belief, will ask for the account of all deeds in this life. So those who engage in destroying any life around them carry the burden of this act into the world after death.

Nūruddīn believed in the sanctity of all life because each thing in the cosmos is a manifestation of one or more attributes of the divine. Such a view is beginning to be appreciated in the current times in the face of the ecological crisis that we face today. Environmental ethicists and activists are pushing for a radical change in how non-human nature is perceived in the contemporary ecology of ideas. The deep ecology movement promotes a bio-centric perspective, which sees both humans and non-humans as part of the earth's community and as such they have the same membership rights.[53] According to this perspective, the natural world exists as an organic whole, in which different parts are interlinked, creating a complex web of life, where the proper functioning of each part is directly or

[53] Naess, pp. 64–84: Fox, pp. 252–61.

indirectly linked to other parts of the web. Each individual organism is thus conceived of as a teleological center of life, pursuing its own good in its own way. In the case of humans as moral agents, the conception of teleological center is linked to our ability to make judgment about the events in the world as good or bad, desirable or undesirable. We make such judgments to promote our own good. However, individual plants and animals can also be seen as teleological centers of life engaged in realizing their own good in their own unique way. This perspective in postmodern ethics is, of course, a good beginning to deal with the ecological crisis, but the problem here is that it shifts the traditional perspective that humans are the center of the universe to the other extreme, which labels each thing in existence as the center of its own universe. Such an approach ignores the fact that humans are the most evolved creatures and hence, must shape their world in more responsible ways, because how they approach their lives and the world around them will deeply impact the environment. The orientation in postmodern thought to reject any absolute reality makes it impossible for western ethical systems to be grounded in any metanarrative of an absolute reality or foundational consciousness that comes before the multiplicity manifested in the universe.

In western tradition, ethics has become a system created by society so all members can live in harmony without infringing on the rights of any other member. Such a system thus works horizontally, where the impetus for goodness is rooted in social interaction with other members of society. This perspective is problematic as the general moral climate of contemporary age is geared towards individualism and consumerism. The scales of nobility that can be recovered from the social mores as a guideline for one's behavior are increasingly tipping downwards to greed and exploitation for individual gain. A need exists for people to transform at the individual level in order to transform the society. As Nasr writes, "For the best way to integrate human society is first of all to be integrated oneself. One cannot do good unless one is good, an all too simple truth so often forgotten in the modern world. Nor can one save others unless one has first been saved oneself. Therefore the method of integration contained in Sufism concerns not only the individuals who are affected by it but also casts its light upon the whole of society."[54]

The Rishī Sufi perspective not only situates the natural world in the Absolute Reality or God or the Necessary Being, which comes before the cosmos, but it also situates ethics in the same reality via the most Beautiful Names of God. According to the hadith, "God is a Hidden Treasure, He created the cosmos to know Himself," so only in actualizing the noble traits in the form of the perfect human can the goal of the cosmos be fulfilled. Humans incorporate within themselves the unity of all divine attributes, which they have potential to actualize, whereas the cosmos manifests the differentiated multiplicity of divine attributes of One God. Thus, there is a symbiotic relationship between the humans and the cosmos. If humans do not live up to their real destiny, which is to move closer to the attributes of the perfect human, the cosmos is also going to suffer, because only humans in the hierarchy of the cosmos have power to act upon their environment. In the modern world, this realization is absolutely crucial in light of the general decay of the moral and natural environment.

Nūruddīn urged people who came to him for guidance to fulfill the pact for which they are created and that is to aspire for moral perfection through giving up base human traits and assuming noble traits like compassion, humility, love, and generosity. He advised them to transform their material existence so they live harmoniously with the broader order of things. He promoted an ethics of responsibility for one's

[54] Nasr, p. 51.

relationship to the community as well as the environment and an aesthetic of purity with respect to one's relationship to God. For these twin reasons, he has been a powerful and positive force in the history of Kashmiri culture that promoted communal harmony for centuries.

Four Eminent Disciples

Nūruddīn Rishī had many disciples, but four of them excelled over others and these were Bamuddīn, Zainuddīn, Latīfuddīn, and Nasruddīn.[55] In a verse, Nuruddīn says:

> Buma, Nasar, Baba Zaina and
> Latif I am adorned with—
> God gave me a necklace with
> a set of gold-bead strands.
> They are mine and I am theirs. (v. 59)

Bamuddīn preferred solitude and avoided the company of worldly people. He became famous for his austerities and established himself in Bamuzu,[56] where he lived in a cave. According to a legend, once when Sultan Ali Shah (1413–20) wanted to see Bamuddīn, the latter insisted that he come to him as an ordinary person and not dressed in royal robes. The Sultan visited him dressed in a simple peasant's outfit. Bamuddīn was not impressed and told the Sultan that even though he had taken off his royal robes, his mind was still preoccupied with the thoughts of his kingdom and hence, he could not benefit from any advice. The Sultan asked him why he was so much against worldly people. Bamuddīn replied that he was not against worldly people, but against worldliness. Towards the end of the meeting, he told the Sultan to never visit him again and when he left, Bamuddīn

---

[55] For a detailed account of disciples, see Rafiqi, pp. 189–248. Also, see Gauhar, pp. 63–64.

[56] Bamuzu is fifteen kilometers to the south-east of Anantnag in Kashmir.

threw away the mat on which the Sultan sat during the meeting.

The most eminent disciple of Nūruddīn was Zainuddīn. In a verse, he says: "My Zaina churns the nectar—He renounced the world with honor. The disciple surpassed his preceptor" (v. 62). Zainuddīn excelled in piety and austerities and is reported to have eaten only once in three days. After spending several years with his teacher, he was sent to 'Aish Maqām, where he lived in a cave on the side of a barren hill. According to a legend, a spring miraculously appeared soon after in the vicinity of the cave. Zainuddīn was exiled to Tibet for two years after he incurred the displeasure of Sultan Zainulābidīn. He was recalled from this exile when the Sultan had a health problem and he was told that he would get well only if Zainuddīn Rishī returned to Kashmir. The Sultan sent his son to Tibet to fetch Zainuddīn and himself went to receive him upon his arrival. Another legend relates when Zainuddin died, his disciples put his coffin in a corner in the cave as he had instructed them to do. However, the next day, they saw that the body had disappeared from the coffin. According to another account, Zainuddīn entered his cave toward the end of his life, closed its mouth, and was never seen again.

Nūruddīn's third disciple Latīfuddīn also observed severe penance. He established himself in Poskar. Once he inquired from his disciple Pīrbāz why the vegetables he was eating tasted tough. Pīrbāz replied that he had used dried rather than fresh vegetables for cooking and hence, the difference in taste. Pīrbāz had made this change because whenever he broke the branches or leaves of living plants, he felt they were bleeding and when he boiled them, he felt they cried in pain. He finally decided not to use fresh vegetables for cooking any longer. Latīfuddīn was so moved by this account that he stopped eating green vegetables for the rest of his life and survived on nuts that had fallen off the trees.

Nasruddīn was Nūruddīn Rishī's favorite disciple. He

stayed with him at Tsrar and became the head of this center on his preceptor's death. Many of Nūruddīn's verses are addressed to Nasruddīn, who accompanied his teacher on his travels to different parts of Kashmir. In a verse addressed to him, Nūruddīn comments on the transitoriness of wealth, glory, and possessions:

In the harems of the khans, where
the good people are sent the other way,
I saw beautiful women singing songs
and removing dust with yakhair dusters.
Today I saw them there hoeing to plant cotton.
Nasr, I saw it—now you go and see. (v. 100)

Nasruddīn was also famous for his austerities. Once he was on a forty-day fast, praying in a cell. He was given four walnuts to bring into the retreat. One day Nūruddīn was standing outside the door and he heard the sound of a walnut being cracked. He shouted out that he had sent Nasruddīn into this retreat to break his ego *(nafs)* and not his walnuts. When the retreat ended, Nasruddīn returned all four walnuts to Nūruddīn, thereby demonstrating that he had lived up to the high standards of his preceptor. Another story relates that he used to break his fast with a drink made of water and ashes. Nūruddīn finally told him to stop taking ashes mixed with water and start taking hundred grains of rice everyday, soon to be followed by twenty grains of rice.

Each of the prominent disciples created their own chain of disciples, who were quite accomplished Rishīs and lived up to their preceptors' high standards. The four main centers of Rishī Sufi activities were Tsrar, Bamuzu, 'Aish-Maqām, and Poskar. The cardinal principles of the order were: "to serve mankind, help the needy, share the burden of the sick, infirm and weak" and "to avoid injuring any living being whether in the form of greenery, insects or animals."[57] Rishī

[57] Gauhar, p. 47.

Sufis rejected family life, abstained from eating flesh, and lived in the countryside. They became famous for their austerities, their healing powers, and their protection of disciples from calamities. They rejected the royal patronage and refused to ally themselves with the administration or get involved in politics. Whatever they received in the evening, they distributed by the next day amongst the needy.[58] The Rishī Sufi order was active for about two hundred years before it lost its distinct identity.

Rishī Tradition and Kashmiri Sufi Poetry

The notion of the Unity of Being or *wahdat al wujūd* present in the Rishī Sufi poetry was already a part of the thought system of various Sufi orders that entered Kashmir in medieval times. This concept particularly found resonance with the Kashmiri imagination that was shaped by the local nondualist Śaiva tradition. It was for this reason that many Sufi poets sometimes conveyed their experiences on the Sufi path in terms of the local tradition, which they referred to as the "shāstra" in their poetry. In beautiful poetry, they presented the experience of their communion with God and the lover's joy and anguish in search of the Beloved. Many of the songs have become a part of the Kashmiri musical repertoire. The poetry of many poets such as Svachha Kral, Shams Faqir, Samad Mir, and Ahad Zargar is very much grounded in the local culture. Even though these poets belonged to different Sufi traditions in Kashmir, their poetry reverberates with the philosophy of the Rishi Sufis.

Svachha Kral (d. 1857) in his poetry reflects on the Unity of God in his suggestive lyrics. In a song that is an imaginary dialogue between the poet and his Friend, he writes:

[58] *Khalil, Rauzātu'l Riyāz*, p. 37, quoted in Rafiqi, pp. 239–40.

I said, "No mystery was there,
  from where did it come?"
He said, "On the path of love it ripened."
I said, "Reveal to me the mystery of love."
He said, "If I did, where would you keep it."
I said, "What is outside and what is inside?"
He said, "What is outside is inside."
I said, "Will you tell me about your station?"
He said, "There is neither day nor night there."
I said, "Can you reveal to me your Being?"
He said, "Remove the veil of your self." [59]

Shams Faqir (d. 1904) was both a poet and a great Sufi and is even regarded as the Rumi of Kashmir. Faqir's poetry is filled with colorful images to convey his experiences. In a poem, he compares the experiences of a traveler on the path to the fate of a moth, who sets out "to seek friendship with the flame" and "only after both [are] burned down do they become one."[60] At another place, the lover's fate is expressed in terms of a black bee's attraction for a flower. Faqir also uses musical metaphors to depict the relationship between the creator and the creation. He refers to "the beautiful sound of drums" that encodes the mystery of the divine reality. Inside the drum, he writes, the drum beat is joined with the drum.

Listen! Pay attention to
  the beautiful sound of the drum.
Listen to its mystery—
Seek refuge with a preceptor.
Inside, the drum is joined with the beat.
So many adepts are bewildered in this state.[61]

---

[59] Svaccha Kral, in Saqi, ed. *Sufi Shāyari,* vol. 1., p. 81.
[60] *Kulliyāt. Shams Faqir,* p. 306.
[61] Ibid., p. 143.

In another poem, the quest is presented as retrieving the pearl from the ocean. The seeker must dive deep within to get the treasure. While commenting on the nothingness of every existent thing, he says: "I am nothing myself—what shall I call myself? I see nothing there and nothing here. I am nothing myself." He continues:

Mystics have knowledge of nothingness.
Without effort, they are near their Self.
Three couples, three friends—
  but the Friend remains the same.
Depthless is your river.
The sparks from the fire
  are burning my forehead.
Not a trace of color on the One
  who colors the world.[62]

In several poems, Faqir refers to the local nondualistic tradition while making references to the Unity of God. In another poem with a broader scope, he says

As undifferentiated unity,
  He is infinite.
After reaching the mystery,
  all else is a play.
In silence—you see his sign.
Hey, mad Shams, not a particle
  is separate from Him.
Aspire for higher experience—
  the curtain will open.[63]

Another Sufi poet of this era was Samad Mir (d. 1959), who too was steeped in the local tradition. His poetry is filled with emotions and beautiful images. Many of the poems

[62] Ibid., p. 155
[63] Ibid., p. 143.

depict the inner journey in terms of the lover's search for the Beloved. There are also references to nothingness. In a poem, he tells people to experience the mystery through listening from the eyes and seeing with the ears. Thus, he says:

He Himself is above and Himself below.
Himself He is the king—
  listening and seeing.
Recognize the truth,
  you will become the truth.
Hear from your eyes—
  then no doubts will remain.
Die while alive, get absorbed
  in the One without the other.[64]

Ahad Zargar (d. 1983) is yet another great Kashmiri Sufi poet whose poetry is filled with local themes and images to convey his experiences. In a poem, he says, in the body that is annihilated burns "the flame of water" and it is the breath that makes the particle of dust come alive with the nature of fire. The lower self's quest for the higher Self is sometimes presented in the form of the lover's search for his Beloved. The lover gets drunk on the suffering caused by the absence of the Beloved. His songs reflect on the experience of renouncing duality and contemplating on the Unity. As He is mixed with each particle, the physical reality is just a shadow of the true reality. In another poem, Zargar takes on the role of the other side to comment on the Unity of Being.

I am the hidden mystery inside and outside.
To whom shall I bow and to whom shall I offer prayer?
I am the strange wonder of the temple and the mosque.
To whom shall I bow and to whom shall I offer prayer?

---

[64] *Kulliyāt. Samad Mir,* p. 132.

I am the primary motion of every particle.
I am at the window and I am at the door.
I am the result of both the visible and the invisible.
I am the purpose of the bowing to the Unity.
I am the great secret of both existence and witness.
Consider me the fullness of the entire ocean.[65]

The above examples show that even though the Rishī order as such lost its distinct identity over the centuries, the tradition was appropriated by Sufi mystics and poets, who felt very connected to the local culture. The Rishi ideas continued to live, especially in the vernacular Sufi poetry, which carried on the indigenous tradition of Rishī Sufi into contemporary times, though more covertly and on a much smaller scale because of the changed political reality in Kashmir.

Nūruddīn Rishī is an integral part of the Kashmiri cultural life in that many Sufi singers and musicians pay him tribute by opening musical events with his verses. He is an honored and beloved figure. His sixth birth centenary was celebrated in 1978 with state honors, which led to a renewed interest in his poetry. In recent times as Sufi shrines became centers of dispute among rival Kashmiri Muslim religious leaders and between Kashmiri Hindus and Muslims, Nūruddīn's shrine in Tsrar Sharif remains a revered place for all Kashmiris.

Conclusion

The narrative of communal harmony is closely linked to the life and teachings of Nūruddīn Rishī and his senior contemporary, Lallā. Lallā's teachings embody Śaiva philosophy and Nūruddīn Rishī's teachings were rooted in the Islamic tradition. Yet both were popular with Muslims

---

[65] *Kulliyāt. Abdul Ahad Zargar*, p. 238.

and Hindus alike because they promoted universal love, religious tolerance, compassion, and nonviolence. They practiced what they preached and they taught the masses in the vernacular language. In folk memory and hagiographical accounts, a number of the same verses are attributed to both Lallā and Nūruddīn. Both rejected religious dogma and orthodoxy. People were attracted to them not only due to their elevated spiritual status, but also because their life was based on a broadly-based vision of peaceful coexistence and compassion for the poor and the needy. Especially valuable is their emphasis on cultivating an attitude of love for the other, whether human, animal, or plant. Both urged people to transform their character in order to come closer to moral perfection, which can serve as the foundation for a more humane, peaceful, and just society. It is such an attitude that is sorely needed to preserve our planet from destruction in the coming decades, as the dominant techno-capitalist narrative pushes us in the opposite direction. As humans increasingly define themselves by what they have rather than by what they are or can be in an interconnected world, it is all the more important to recover holistic narratives that promote peaceful coexistence rooted in positive cosmologies.

Nūruddīn Rishī's Verses

Key to Pronunciation of the Romanized Kashmiri Verses

A. Vowels

		Kashmiri Sounds		
a	as in but or 'cut'	akh	اکھ	ا
ā	as in 'father'	āv	او	آ
ä	as in 'bird'	mäj	مٲج	ٲ
ạ	as in 'about'	ạchh	أچھ	أ
i	as in 'it' or 'in'	dil	دِل	اِ
ī	as in 'see'	shīn	شِین	ای
o	as in 'hot'	dŏyum	دوِیم	او
ō	as in 'fort'	pōsh	پوٗش	اوٗ
ŏ	'wa'as in 'water'	sŏn	سوٚن	وٚ
u	as in 'full'	kus	کُس	اُ
ū	as in 'rule'	myūṭh	میوٗٹھ	اوٗ
ü		süti	سٕتِی	اٟ
ei	as in 'may'	āsei	آسے	ے
ai	as in 'lie' or 'tie'	kartai	کرٕتۍ	اۍ

B. Consonants

t	ت	ts	ژ
th	تھ	tsh	ژھ
ṭ	ٹ	ch	چ
ṭh	ٹھ	chh	چھ
d	د		
ḍ	ڈ		

Reflection

1

nafasai myōn chhu mada höstū
amiy hasitī dyutanas tal
krei karövnas rostū
röṭnas kyā chhum chal
sāsas manz akhā lostū[1]
na ta särī hĕtin tal

My ego is a mad elephant.
The elephant has
  crushed me underneath,
    emptying me of good deeds.
Caught am I—powerless.
Only one in a thousand escapes.
All others are trampled.

2

vuduy äsith nĕsar peyam
nafas kuni karār heyam mo vai
halāl trävith harām kheyam
dargāh zāt (zānh) tī preyam[2] *mo vai*

Awake, I fell asleep.
Alas! Restless am I everywhere.
Rejecting the permissible,
  I ate the impermissible.
Alas! Never did I cherish
  the sanctuary within.

---

[1] from lasun: to flourish or to escape the clutches of the ego. The line suggestively conveys that only very few escape the clutches of the ego and make progress on the spiritual path.

[2] to love or hold in affection, Grierson, vol. II, p. 774.

3

nafasī käram adal ta vadal
nafas myōn shetānas badal āv
nafas mānahĕm krei händi kadal
nafas myōn dozakhas badal āv

My ego has caused me confusion.
My ego has taken the place of devil.
I wish my ego accepted
the path of good deeds.
My ego has taken the place of hell.

4

zuvo tsa boztō kanavān
yi ho marinani khabar shinvān[3] *chhai*
käli handis zan ninai pujavān
yi gāsa käni[4] *duniyahich bramvān*[5] *chhai*

Hey, self, listen carefully—
the news of death creates emptiness.
In due time, you will be taken
like a sheep to the butcher's shop.[6]
The mortal body is illusory.

---

[3] emptiness.
[4] gāsu kān: literal meaning, grass body; metaphoric meaning, mortal body
[5] from bram: delusion or illusion. Grierson, vol. I, p. 123; bramvān: illusory.
[6] The reference here is to the finality of death over which nobody has control.

5

prenis badnas malyun dāg gom
zāg[7] *gōm nīrith bāga andarei*
hārni[8] *garimiy pōh ta māg*[9] *gōm*
phāh gōm nīrith hara bandarei[10]
zazarani[11] *chhŏka hani hani dāh*[12] *gōm*
gonāh gäm tsäri ta kahi ubrei
myūth ta mödur khĕth unda syāh gōm
nāh[13] *gōm pānas rāh*[14] *kas karei*

Stained with impurity is my fair body.
The bird has slipped out of the garden.
The hot summer has turned into
  the mid-winter.
Drained of warmth is my body.
Old age has wasted me slowly.
Bad deeds have I piled up—
  how will I rise?
Eating the delicious and tasty has
  turned my insides black.
I am lost—
  Who can I ask for help?

---

[7] a crow or, in this case, a bird. The "bird" here stands for the higher Self and the "garden" the heart.
[8] hār: mid summer (the month of July).
[9] pōh ta māg: mid winter (months of December and January).
[10] bandare: trading town, Grierson, p. 112, vol. I; hara: God; the body as the city of God is a medium to come closer to the divine reality.
[11] to wither away as in old age.
[12] dāh gatshun: burn from within or become wasted.
[13] nāh gōṃ pānas: self becoming naught.
[14] rāh karun: to ask for help.

6

sŏndari kāmadivun chāv gōm
yāvun yām gōm pōshanmötū
sangaruk[15] *shīn ta wŏluruk vāv*[16] *gōm*
muhith ṭhag gōm akahötū[17]
wulagi batas[18] *kana ta tŏh gōm*
garības dŏh gōm variyas yötū

Filled with desires was my fair body—
beguiled by beautiful things
I spent my youth.
My experience now is like that of
the chill of a mountain glacier and
a turbulent storm in the Wular.
The robber has robbed me of all.[19]
The fragrant rice tastes
like the unhusked grain and chaff.
A day stretches into
a year for my poor self.

---

[15] sangar: a steep mountain; sangaruk shīn: the literal meaning here is "mountain snow," which on steep mountains at high altitudes turns into glaciers.
[16] The Wular is the largest fresh-water lake in India. It is situated at a distance of about 50 kilometers northwest of Srinagar. In the windy or stormy weather, the surface of the lake turns turbulent with rolling waves. See Sufi, pp. 158–159, n. 3.
[17] all at once.
[18] wulag bata: a kind of fragrant rice, Grierson, vol. II, p. 1113.
[19] "robber" symbolizes here the lower self, which robbed him of good deeds by directing his attention to the fulfillment of desires, rather than to performing good deeds with detachment.

7

shoga tsali nīrith panzĕra mŏtsĕm[20]
lot lot tulnam hāhākār
vodur tati vili pōsh zan hatĕm
bār khudāyā pāph nĕvār

When the parrot escapes,
  the cage will remain.[21]
Gently will they lament for me.
My body will wither away
  like a delicate flower.
Great God!! Absolve me of sins.

8

zuva kandi röchhmakh darad sŏn zan
tsei kuni zan mŏlay na drōy
välith tshünanai ḍāyan gazan bŏn zan
tati lūni[22] *zen panini kämai*

O, Body, I took care of you
  like the gold from Darad.[23]
Your value did not manifest at all.
After being wrapped,
  you will be buried under
    two and a half yards of earth.
You will collect your wages there.[24]

---

[20] Saqi (p. 146) uses the word "maṭhĕm" instead of "mŏtsem" in the verse, while Afaqi's transcription (p. 295) "mŏtsem" used here makes more sense in this context.
[21] The "parrot" symbolizes the soul and the "cage" the body.
[22] from lōne: to reap or to collect.
[23] the territory generally around the north of Kashmir, Grierson, vol. I, p. 241.
[24] "to collect wages" after death in this verse means that the fruits of one's actions, both good and bad, are reaped by the individual in the hereafter.

9

nafasī lōgum̀ nārav krötshū[25]
dama dama möngnam kötsh hō
sarahan bugī dih gōm ötshū
bugī sŏrun götsh hō
samsāras āyās pāntsh dŏh pötshū
gäm yīra gāv tīr vötsh hō[26]

My ego is like a poker
for shoveling out hot coal.
Every moment it asks for more.
My body is too weak to remember God.
Remember God I must.
As a transient guest I have come
to the world—I have lost all.

10

sŏnas ta sartali akuy zalun[27]
tī ḍīshith zuv myon kalan hyöt[28]
ḍyūnṭhum nundĕn lyuth[29] *ta ḍiṭhĕn*[30] *phŏlun*
tavai andvan mĕ tsalun hyöt

The gold and the brass look alike—
On seeing that, I began to reflect.
I saw the good suffer and the wicked flourish.
So I started retreating into the backwoods.

---

25 nār krötsh: a poker to shovel out hot coal.
26 literal meaning: my cow, sheep, and calf are all drowned; metaphoric meaning: I have lost all.
27 akuy zalun: same appearance.
28 kalan hyöt: began to reflect.
29 to suffer travail or humiliation, Grierson, vol. I, p. 545.
30 wicked; harsh natured, Grierson, vol. I, p. 258.

Solitude

11

ādana par laban zōgum[31]
chhuvum ta lōgum pahalvān[32]
tsandun tsaṭith arkhöl sögum[33]
mārkhŏr[34] *pata lögum shetān*
dāh bäts rachhām süti küntsh na lögum
tī ḍūṭh körum[35] *ta mōrum pān*

In my youth, obsessed was I
  with the outer world.
Enjoying myself,
  I acted as a hero.
After chopping off the sandalwood tree,
  I watered the arkhol[36] tree.
The devil pursued my lower self
  filled with desires.
Many family members I raised,
  nobody remains with me.
Having realized that—
  I controlled my ego.

---

[31] par laban zōgum: preoccupied with the outer world, rather than looking within oneself.
[32] a champion or a hero.
[33] sandalwood.
[34] khŏr: an eater, Grierson, vol. 1, p. 409; mārkhŏr: an eater of desires or the desiring one.
[35] to perceive, to observe, or to realize.
[36] The arkhol tree has drooping branches like that of the ash tree. Its branches cause blisters when touched, Grierson, vol. I, p. 43. In this verse, the fragrant sandalwood tree (symolizing the higher Self), believed to have healing properties, is contrasted with the arkhol tree (symbolizing the lower self), which entangles people in the transitory material reality that is full of suffering.

12

damī huhei gōm damī huha gōm
damī muh gōm[37] *muhith kath*
damī akuy kadam kruh[38] *gōm*
damī säh gōm sotith kath

One moment I inhaled
and another moment I exhaled.[39]
My attachment disappeared instantly.
In a moment one step became a mile.
My [ego]-tiger became weak instantly.

13

tsyūnum[40] *gunum*[41] *tshōrum*[42] *ta gōrum*
praktsa vih ahōrum[43] *mĕ*
duhli dubas nafas mōrum
gār ahōrum ta sörum dai

I meditated, I remembered,
I searched, and I reflected.
I sacrificed the poison
of my animal nature.
With conscious effort,
I restrained my ego.
I renounced my home and
remembered God.

---

[37] muh gatshun: delusion to depart or true knowledge to be aquired, Grierson, vol. I, p. 553.

[38] a measure of distance, Grierson, vol. I, p. 469.

[39] The reference here is to breathing exercises to focus the mind and achieve an inward-directed state to open oneself to the higher Self.

[40] from tsēnun: to meditate.

[41] gunum (from ganun or ganyōv): to firmly fix, Grierson, vol. I, p. 292.

[42] tshōrum (from tshāndun or tshārun): to search.

[43] from aharan: to offer as sacrifice, Grierson, vol. I, p. 18.

14

andvan rūzith kand kopävüm[44]
aval mĕ na banōvum gŏphei
unda mal kaḍith darshan dyōvum
qabri hünz lahad hävüm gŏphei
kŏṇga ta kōfūr tan nävüm
äshvanich prakath sävüm gophei

Living in backwoods,
I made my body
tremble in fear.[45]
First, I made a cave—
After removing inner impurities,
I made Him reveal Himself.
I turned the cave into my grave.
With saffron and camphor[46]
I purified my body.
My desire for good things
I put to sleep in the cave.

15

bugi tseti kal gäyī myänī
gōsai boh gäli gäli tsamith kath
ava voni boh ta kal trāv na chänī
yām hankal gatshĕm tsämith kath

God is within—
The devotion is mine.
Little by little I have withered away.
Now I will not let go
of your devotion until
the door is unbolted.

---

[44] tremble in fear, Grierson, vol. II, p. 1057.
[45] Here, "tremble in fear" refers to Nuruddin's state of mind when he rounouced his family and the support of the social network.
[46] "saffron" and "camphor" symbolize stages of purification on the Sufi path.

16

dŏhas guzōrum näphla[47] *'hathā*
rātas rūdus zāgei
yödvoni karham köbūliyathā
na ta hūn zan phyūrus āgei[48]

Daytime I offered
hundreds of prayers.
In the night,
I maintained my vigil.
May you accept my prayers now—
Otherwise, O, Lord,
I am like a stray dog.

17

rātas dŏhas kälimā[49] *pörum*
tī zan mörum tilki sŏn[50]
rāth ta dŏh kani pĕṭh börum[51]
ŏsus sās ta sapanus sŏn

I recited the sacred formula
day and night—
I became absorbed in it.
My stone-heart I soaked in it
day and night—
From ashes, I became gold.

---

[47] supererogatory prayers as opposite to obligatory prayers.
[48] master or lord, Grierson, vol. I, p. 16.
[49] the "kalima" is the mystic formula that encapsulates the Islamic faith of monotheism: "there is no god, but God."
[50] the literal meaning of this line is that he rubbed the "kalima"' like gold to the middle of the forehead. The metaphoric meaning is that he became absorbed in the sacred words of the "kalima."
[51] Nūruddīn refers to the worldly people as stone-hearted. Here, the use of the expression "kani pĕṭh börum" could convey the meaning of permeating the ordinary stone-heart with the sacred mystic formula.

18

yeti ti mĕ tsäi tati ti mĕ tsäi
mĕ tsäi kartam gulzār
sōruy trävith rötukh mĕ tsäi
mĕ tsäi hāvtam dīdār

I depend on you
both here and there—
make my rose garden bloom.[52]
Renouncing all,
I have caught hold of you—
reveal Yourself to me.

19

tas padmān pōrachi lalei
tami galei amrĕth piva
tami shiv vuchh thalei thalei[53]
tyuth mĕ var dito diva

That Lalla of
Padmānpura—
She drank nectar
by mouthfuls.
She saw Śiva everywhere.
O, Lord, bestow such a boon on me.

---

[52] The blooming of the rose garden symbolizes opening of the heart to mystic revelation.
[53] In the Afaqi collection, the third line of this verse (p. 598, vol. 2) is transcribed as "sva sänī avatār lalei" which can be translated as "She is our avatār Lallā." Also, see Saqi, p. 148, n. 1.

20

luka bavanachi kajei
äkajei[54] *karan siva*
süti jānāvāran tsajei
tyuth mĕ var dito diva

The mute woman
of Luka Bhavan[55]—
She worshipped God
with total absorption.
With birds she flew away.
O, Lord, bestow such a boon on me.

21

ḍanḍak vanaki zalaka reshī
katsh phala karĕn siva
pŏkhta bakhti ōs mukhat suy
tyuth mĕ var dito diva

Zalaka Rishī of
the Ḍanḍak forest—
He survived on
the fruit of wild shrubs.
A sincere devotee,
he had self-realization.
O, Lord, bestow such a boon on me.

---

[54] single-mindedly or with the whole attention.
[55] Luka Bhavan is a place in Anantnag district in Kashmir.

22

resh vanaki mīrān reshī
tsandara sāsas ann-zal[56] *chava*
ada düyi rös akāsh gövuy
tyuth mĕ var dito diva

Mīrān Rishī of
  the Rishi forest—
He lived for a
  thousand lunar months.
Without duality,
  he went to heaven.
O, Lord, bestow such a boon on me.

23

khōri[57] *röstuy jahāza tōrum*
mōrum mad lūb ta muh
sĕdi·vönda rahith sahĕb gōrum
ada prazanovum panun ruh

Without an oar,
  I ferried the boat across.
I killed pride, greed, and attachment.
With devotion, I searched for the Lord—
  only then I recognized my higher Self.

---

[56] The word "anzul" in this verse in the Saqi collection (p. 149) is transcribed in the Parimoo collection (v. 114) as "ann-zal." The latter transcription used here makes more sense.The expression "ann-zal cheva" means "ate and drank" or in other words "lived."

[57] oar.

24

yeti ti mĕ tsäi tati ti mĕ tsäi
me tsai tshārān lūstum[58] *dŏh*
gyānas manz yeli röṭukh mĕ tsäi
mĕ tsa ta pānas ditum tshŏh[59]

Both here and there
  I depend on you.
I spent the day looking for you.
In meditation when I became
  absorbed in you—
I found myself in bliss.

---

[58] from lōsun: to come to an end, Grierson, vol. I, p. 534.
[59] tshōh dyun: to cause to feel unbounded rapture or happiness, Grierson, vol. II, p. 1057.

Love

25

boh chhus akuy süti götshum yār
yāras süti dama dama paka
yārnai ḍeshan gul gatshĕm khār
yeti myōn yār tati myōn makka

Alone am I—
  I yearn to be with my Friend.
Every moment I want to be with Him.
Without my Friend,
  flowers will turn into thorns.
Wherever my Friend is,
  there is my Mecca.

26

yemi hyöt tihandi bartal zāgun
tas panuni sharbath pāna chāvei
chhis päthür byön byön akuy chhu māgun[60]
su yas ṭoṭhi ta suy ada prāvei

Whoever starts a vigil at His door,
He offers him His own
  nectar to drink.
A variety of plays—
  Only one is the Director.
Whom He loves,
  he is the one who attains.

---

[60] stage director.

27

hihuai türi ta hihuai tätei
hanzei[61] *karēs lŏy ta gŏy*[62]
'āshaq chhi nisār tahänzi vatei
yeti bömbras ta pōsh āsī khŏy
tī yas vĕd sani suy ada matei
tas ada gatshī dŏyī aköy

Alike in the cold and the heat,
steadily engaged in practice,
lovers sacrifice themselves on His path
where the black bee is attracted to the flower.
He who absorbs this knowledge—
for him, the two are united.[63]

28

su mĕ nishei boh tas nishei
mĕ tas nishei karār āv
nahakai tshōnḍum mĕ pardīshei
pananei dīshei mĕ yār āv

He is near me and
I am near Him—
I found peace near Him.
Wrongly, I looked for Him
in the outer world.
I found my Friend in the inner world.

---

[61] The word 'hanzei' comes from the phrase "hanze panze rōzun": to keep onself in good state. Here, it means "a steady state," Grierson, vol. I, p. 341.

[62] lŏy ta gŏy: engaged in practice, Grierson, vol. I, p. 543.

[63] The reference here is to the Unity of Being. Worldly people identify themselves strongly with their ego and hence, experience themselves as separate from the divine reality. Those who seek God through love, they experience some aspects of the divine reality in the manifest cosmos.

29

'alim chhuy söndūkas sŏn zan barun
sivas sōdā pakun pava
sodā muts chhuy pöz azmāvun
īmān tsōng chhuy rachhun vāva
namāz chhai zamīni phal zan vavun
adab chhuy nund papī tava
dil chhuy gāḍ hŏkh mo trāvun
zikri hund pōni dis lasī tava
nafas chhuy lāl atha mo trāvun
sahĕb chhu māshōk tōshī tava

Aquiring knowledge is like
   filling gold in a chest.
The service bargain is to follow the path.
The agreement is not so much
   to test the truth.
Honesty is like a lamp:
   protect it from the wind.
Praying is like sowing seeds in the earth.
Reverence is good:
   they will ripen with that.
Heart is a fish:
   don't leave it dry.
Irrigate it with the remembrance of God:
   it will flourish then.
The self is a jewel: don't lose it.
Lord is the Beloved:
   He will thus be pleased.

30

kamsanā nĕndrihatī vudī
kamsanā nĕshibŏdī byŏn
kamsanā lola 'ashkani dädī
kamsanā sās ta kamsanā sŏn
kamsanā marnas brōnṭhai mūdī
äsī sās ta sapanī sŏn

Some are awake while heavy-eyed.
Some are disconnected due to ignorance.
Some burn in the fire of love.
Some are ashes and some are gold.
Some die before their death[64]—
from ashes, they turn into gold.

31

āshkan tresh ta bŏchi na āsei
kāshak kamis pati yiyna zāt (zānh)
chhu duras vatan sadfas nishei
tsūras nĕndar āsi na zāt (zānh)

Lovers are neither hungry nor thirsty.
Those without love wait for the one
who will never come.[65]
The pearl's place is in the oyster—
The [ego]-thief never gets sleepy. [66]

[64] The expression "dying before death" means that one's desire for material things is extinguished through conscious cultivation of an attitude of detachment towards the world.

[65] The first two lines refer to the difference between two types of seekers: those who seek God through love and hence, experience some aspects of Him in His manifest attributes and those who reject such experience and only use their intellect to understand God in His dissimilarity.

[66] In Sufi poetry the "pearl" is a metaphor for the Beloved or the Lord, the personalized form of the Divine, and the "oyster" symbolizes the lover's heart. The lower self or the ego is always on the lookout to distract the seeker from this experience. He must thus be vigilant so he does not lose the "pearl" in the heart.

32

boh päri kāngri ta jandas
yemi vandas kärüm türi rächhī
bahū ta bahūmat nyāmüts vandas
nūn ta sädarkanz chhum yaḍ rächhī
boh kyā mangai qalayi qandas
hand ta hākh chhum chhöt mänchhī
bugi mehrā[67] *tshüntam vŏndas*
dĕv bandas gatsham sharmi rächhī

I love my kangari[68] and
my patched robe, which
protect me from the winter cold.
Blessings are in abundance
in the winter.
Salted sadarkanz[69] fills my stomach.
No need do I have
for sugar candy.
Chicory and leafy greens
are my white honey.
Lord, bestow your grace
on my heart.
So your servant is protected
from dishonor.

---

67 from mihra: benevolence, kindness, grace, or mercy.
68 A small clay pot full of hot coal, encased in a wicker basket with handles, which Kashmiris use to warm themselves in the winter.
69 A sweetend sour drink made from fermented rice.

33

māshōkan yeli darshun hōvun
darshun dyovun mansūrasai
shōkuk sharāb su yeli chōvun
qatal karövnas zan tsūrasai
kōng ta kostūra tati yeli nōvun
man ma nōvun tami dārsai
'āshkan 'ärifan vathā hävan
kathā thävan samsārsai

When He appeared to his beloveds,
  a vision He sent to Mansur.
He got him drunk on the wine of love
  and had him murdered like a thief.[70]
When Mansur was purified there
  with saffron and musk,[71]
    his heart filled with joy at that door.
He showed the path to lovers and saints—
  stories were left for the world.

---

[70] The reference here is to Mansūr Al-Hallāj, the famous Persian Sufi mystic and poet, who in his mystic trances would utter the words "Ana al-Haqq" (I am the Truth), which the orthodox religious authorities believed was a blasphemy. Mansur was publicly executed in 922.

[71] "saffron and musk" symbolize experiences of purification on the Sufi path.

34

chharā pyeyāyas[72] *kavsana tsäjin*
mansūr kākas vuha näjan gayei
shānti hänz krei kĕth syod väjin
andrächa äs ta nĕbar kath pĕyei

He had sudden realization,
he could not bear it.
Mansur was set on fire.
A tranquil state he
experienced spontaneously.
It was not meant to be exposed.

35

karto krei ta yehto pĕnjei[73]
murkho bōzto ranjavith[74]
'āshakav pul ta pätav ganjei
yāvun muḍas tsöl riṇzavith[75]

Perform good deeds and
observe spiritual discipline.
Fool, listen with gratitude.
Lovers fastened their sandals.
The fool's youth slipped away unnoticed.[76]

---

[72] chhara pyeyāyas: to descend with sudden force.
[73] from pĕnḍu: a house altar, Grierson, vol. II, p. 738 & 740; yehto pĕnje: to observe spiritual discipline.
[74] from ranzun: to be gratified, comforted, or consoled, Grierson, vol. II, p. 839.
[75] from rinzun: to escape or flee away secretly, Grierson, vol. II, p. 839.
[76] The reference here is to two types of people, those filled with love for God and devoted to spiritual practice, and those who waste their youth engaged in the fulfillment of worldly desires.

36

yim kas mārith māran
tim tsālan ta lāgan dās
yim sahaza khudāy gāran
tim sōruy vĕndan sās

After killing the lower self,
  those who become disciplined,
    they suffer and act as servants.
Searching for God truthfully,
  they consider everything as ashes.

37

'āshaq suy yus 'ashqa süti dazī
sŏn zan prazalĕs panun pān
'āshaqun dōd yas vālinji sazī
suy ada vātī lāmakān

A lover burns with love—
He shines like gold.
He whose heart is afflicted with love—
  he is the one who will be
    joined with the higher Self.

38

sahaz gyān yava süti ulangī[77]
lolaki khambai rangī zāth
āsi man milävith tan sāda ḍangī[78]
yatshei patshei mangī bāth[79]
düy yöd tsalyĕs kāsyĕs bangī
tas kus ada rangī zāth

The true knowledge emerges
from that, which permeates
one's nature with love.
If the heart is united and
the body is pure and steady,
it willingly and faithfully
seeks guidance.
When duality is gone,
the confusion is removed.
Who else will then manifest
as one's nature?[80]

[77] to emerge or to realize.
[78] ḍangi or ḍanji: healthy, firm.
[79] means or plan, Grierson, vol. I, p. 139. In this specific usage, it refers to spiritual means or guidance.
[80] The reference here is to those who purify themselves and open their heart so it is permeated with love, which in its purest form is an attribute of God.

Unity

39

khudāy chhu akuy nāv chhäs lachhā
zikri rös akh kachhā mō
vumbar vĕndun akuy pachhā
rizka rös akh machhā mō

God is One—
His names are many.
Not a blade of grass exists
without remembering Him.
Consider life a fortnight.
Not even a fly exists
without His sustenance.

40

yus ōs yeti suy chhuy tatei
suy chhuy prath shāyi raṭith makān
suy chhuy pyāda ta suy chhuy rathei
suy chhuy sōruy gupith pān

He who is here
is also there.
He is omnipresent.
He is the soldier and
He is the chariot.
Himself hidden—
He is omnipotent.

41

gyān yas vötaran[81] *tas täjī*
su kari haras tsĕti bāv
mad yas mor ta khudī tsäjī
boh na kunh ta mĕ kyā nāv
su yemi ḍyūnṭh duyi tas tsäjī
ada kus kari kŏnd ta grāv

In whom the knowledge dawns, he knows—
He devotedly remembers God.
He who kills pride and renounces the ego [says]—
"I am nobody and I have no name."
He who experiences Him,
his duality fades away.
Who will then criticize and complain?[82]

42

kunirai bōzakh kuni nā rōzakh
ami kuniran kotāh dyut jalāv
aqal ta fikir tōr kot sōzakh
kami māli chĕth hyok su dariyāv

If you realize the One,
the self will disappear.
So much brilliance emanates from the One.
Intellect and anxiety have no place there.
Who could drink from that river, my dear?

---

[81] dawns.

[82] This verse brings together several ideas, the first is that those who renounce their ego and open their hearts to the divine reality, they become receptacles of spiritual wisdom. The second idea is that such people are without any pride because they have submitted themselves to the divine will and hence, erased to a great extent the sense of duality that the ordinary people feel with their strong sense of ego. And as such, they have no need to criticize or complain.

43

'alimuk āgur kalimuk mānei
krei hund āgur mĕ na khan[83]
shunyihuk āgur pānai zānei
södruk āgur labĕs na tshĕn

The sacred formula[84] is
the source of knowledge.
Renouncing the ego is
the source of good deeds.
The source of the void
He knows Himself.
Uninterrupted is
the source of the ocean.

44

bugi päri päri chāni qōdrätsei
zōnuth yas yuth dyututh tas tyuth avakāth
sahiba päri chāni märifatsei
dyututh rasūl khudāyas moijizāth

God, I adore your creation.
As you know an entity
so you bestow on it its status.[85]
Lord, I adore your divinity.
You gave the Prophet (Muhammad)
the power of miracles.

---

[83] khan: to dig; me na khan: not entrenched in the ego.
[84] See Verses, n. 49.
[85] According to Muslim belief, each entity before it comes into existence is nonexistent in the all ecompassing knowledge of God. When the light of God falls on it, it comes to life to enjoy its attributes.

45

pānai chhu gindān nafī isbātas[86]
akis sātas labĕs na tshĕn
arāyish[87] *ditsün pratha sifātas*
zātas löbun na marun ta zĕn
sharaf bakhshun hazrat insānas
trukuy chhukh ta pānay tsĕn
sōruy pānay vuchhakh kyā pānas
rātas labi na nĕndar ta khĕn
timav na dyān kör atha gyānas
änis chhu hihuy rāth ta dĕn

He Himself plays the reality of totality
  without a moment of interruption.
He adorns every attribute.
No birth or death for the Essence.
A superior place is
  bestowed on humans.[88]
If you are wise,
  you will meditate on the Self.
He is everywhere—
  you are nowhere.
No sleep or food in the night.[89]
They paid no attention to this knowledge.
Day and night are the same to the blind.

---

[86] The mystic formula or sacred teaching. See Verses, n. 49.
[87] adornment.
[88] The reference here is to the position of humans at the top of the hierarchy of creation, because they have been blessed with the potential to realize all God's attributes or names as stated in the Koranic verse—"God taught Adam all names" (2:31).
[89] This line suggestively conveys that a sincere devotee remembers God day and night, without any need for sleep or food.

46

dyututh naras gōr ta tularis mānchhī
dyututh hulam halis rōṇṭhanas dachh
bugi pärī chāni qudrätsei
dyututh rūsis[90] köstūrī[91] rachh[92]

You gave sweetness to the man
  and honey to the bee.
You gave grapes to the twisted creeper.
Lord, I adore your creation.
You entrusted the antelope with musk.

47

aval alif kunuy allāh
avala pata äkhar zi vālan tas
baei gōv muhammad rasūl allāh
qayāmüts shafa't kar umatas

The first letter 'alif' represents one God.
He permeates all from the first to the last.
And Muhammad is the messenger of God.
On the resurrection day, He will intercede
  on behalf of his followers.

---

[90] a kind of black antelope or the musk deer, Grierson, vol. II, p. 842.
[91] musk, Grierson, vol. I, p. 483.
[92] protection or guardianship, Grierson, vol. II, p. 824.

48

ādam vopadȯvun sŏbāva mětsei
metsi hündi kar[93] *gänḍith kath*
sāri nyāmats vopdāvěn metsei
ranān metsivěn bānan kěth
zuv tsali nīrith mör mŏtsi mětsei
mětsei měts gatshi mīlith kath

He created man with the earthly nature
and shaped him in the frame of clay.
He created all natural things from clay.
Cooking is done in pots of clay.
When life leaves,
the body is reduced to dust.
Dust gets mixed with dust.

49

buha bayi sütī ta shěrdār[94] *trōvum*
sāri vumbari chhäviim aküy kānth
sahaza zala yeli sharīr nōvum
bihith sär körum aikānth

From the fear of the world,
I renounced the evil ways.
To only one Lord I devoted all life.
When I purified my body
in the water of truth,
I roamed sitting in solitude.

---

[93] "kar" is from "akār" (Skt): form.
[94] shěr: wickedness, Grierson, vol. II, p. 889; shěrdār: evildoing.

50

yakh tulkatur ta shīn[95]
byön byön päda kör āshen
yāmath khötukh pūri kani rav
tāmath timan treyan akuy gav

Ice, icicles and snow—
God created them as different.
As the sun rises in the east
the three are turned into one.

51

pānai pānas pāph nĕvarei
yus nunda sanzun döp hĕyei
düyi vasith chhuy apōr tarun
akh kārana ta bĕyi krei

He absolves himself of his sins
who adopts Nund Sanz's teachings.
By transcending duality,
you must go across.
Only One is the cause and
the action follows.

[95] yakh: ice; tulkatur: icicles; shīn: snow.

Unveiling

52

voni gāsh ḍyūnṭhum vana ketha gaṭa
babri langas dapa sŏyi kath
diluk darvāza ketha māli vaṭa
sŏnas ketha dima kātsuk vāṭh
khŏdāy ḍyūnṭhum kas māli khaṭa
jānas süti chhum jān sangāṭh

I saw Light—
  I cannot call it darkness.
A sprig of sweet basil,
  I cannot call nettle.
My heart's door, I cannot close.
Glass I cannot use to solder gold.
I experienced the Lord—
  I cannot hide.
Joined with the Self is my self.

53

yim unda shŏd darshana gālī
tim nĕbra zäri ta kälī chhī
yim drāy tava nār shahalī
tim ada lāl mŏlalī chhī

Those who dissolve in
  the sacred vision within,
    act deaf and dumb on the outside.
Unscathed they emerge from the fire.[96]
Priceless jewels thus they are.

---

[96] The reference here is to the fire of hell.

54

aval reshī ahmad reshī
döyum uwais qarnī āv
treyum reshī zalak reshī
tsuryum hazrat palās āv
pūntsyum reshī rumai reshī
sheyum hazrat mīrān āv
satim kärüm dash na hishī
boh nai künh ta mĕ kyā nāv

Ahmad[97] Rishī was the first Rishī—
Uwais Qaran, the second, followed.
Zalak Rishī was the third Rishī—
Hazrat Palās, the fourth, followed.
Rumi Rishī was the fifth Rishī—
Hazrat Mīrān, the sixth, followed.
The seventh did not attain the same state —
I am nobody and I have no name.[98]

55

path yim reshī bövī
timan taph tajäkh ta kyāi
vyöndukh[99] *zuv ta mör yivai*
kar bandan tōshi khudāy

The Rishīs of the past—
they knew how to do penance.
They offered their body and soul to God.
May God be pleased with his servants!

---

[97] The reference here is to Prophet Muhammad.

[98] Nūruddīn compares himself to other historical or unknown figures and with humility acknowledges that he belongs to the same lineage but has yet to attain their high spiritual status.

[99] from vandun: to devote, offer, Grierson, vol. II, p. 1123.

56

yötuy bas nāzi[100] *ādam köranas*
sōri rahmäts böranas sar tā pāy
khoshhāl chhus zĕnas ta marnas
chhus boh tasund banda su myōn khudāy
aräyish ditsün phalkas ta dartas[101]
umäts amīn sūzun rasūl khudāy
umīdvār chhus tati ubarnas
yeti owais qaran chhum rāhnumai[102]

When He proudly named him Adam,
He filled him with mercy
from head to foot.
Happy am I alive or dead.
I am His servant and
He is my Lord.
He adorned the sky and the earth—
a trustworthy apostle
He sent to his followers.
I am hopeful of rising there.
Uwais Qaran is my guide here.

---

[100] bas karun: to have done, Grierson, vol. I, p. 131; nāzi: proudly.
[101] phalkas ta dartas: the sky and the earth.
[102] guide.

57

pōshamatĕn[103] *yiman abdālan*
khŏsh kaliman būzukh mānei
gosh rŏṭukh pĕṭh sangāṭhan
yiman lālan mŏl kus zānei

Divinely intoxicated, those spiritually elevated—
They grasp the meaning of sacred words.
In assembly, they maintain their silence.
Nobody knows the value of these jewels.

58

tshānjām bavanan[104] *bĕyi shĕn dishen*
neib ta nishāna[105] *lōbmas na kunei*
pritshām[106] *mala-bāban ta tapa-reshan*
tim lagi būzi būzi revānei[107]
dab yeli dyutamas fikiran[108] *ta andeishan*[109]
ada suy ḍyūnṭhum boh na kunei

I searched for Him in different worlds and
in six directions.
Not a trace did I find anywhere.
I asked Mullahs and ascetics—
They were annoyed to hear
my questions again and again.
When I let go of my thoughts and doubts,
I saw Him pervading all—
and I was nowhere.

---

[103] from pōshamotu, literal meaning: passionate lover of flowers, Grierson, vol. II, p. 778; metaphoric meaning: those imbued with divine madness or divinely intoxicated.
[104] metaphysical or spiritual realities.
[105] neib ta nishāna: trace, Grierson, vol. I, p. 619.
[106] to ask.
[107] from rivun: to be distraught, Grierson, vol. II, p. 853.
[108] reflection, thought.
[109] doubts.

59

buma nasur ta bāba zänu
latīf rambavunū[110] *chhus*
khudāy ditsām tröṭa[111] *sömbräno*[112]
yimay myäni boh yihnduy chhus

Buma, Nasar, Baba Zaina and
  Latif I am adorned with—
God gave me a necklace with
  a set of gold-bead strands.
They are mine and I am theirs.

60

suy tsāli nĕnda yemi vöv byolū
tshänḍith kadĕs hāma käni
sonta yemi vöv harada tami tōlū
suy tsāv jantas lägith väni

One who sows seeds,
  endures the weeding process.
Searchingly, he pulls out
  weeds and old branches.
One who sows in spring,
  weighs in autumn.
He enters heaven as a trader.[113]

---

[110] to be adorned with, Grierson, vol. II, p. 834.
[111] a necklace of several strands adorned with moonshaped gold beads, Grierson, vol. II, p. 1032.
[112] Saqi (v. 322) has transcribed this line as "khudāy ditsām tirtha su madāno." Afaqi's transcription (p. 562, vol. 2) used here makes more sense.
[113] Nūruddīn uses activities involved in planting a crop as a metaphor for different stages on the Sufi path. Thus, sowing the seeds of good thoughts and actions, and purifying oneself through removing negative character traits eventually leads to the accumulation of good deeds. Just as a farmer during the harvest season trades his harvested crop for monetary value, similarly a spiritually engaged individual accumulates merit in this world to be exchanged on death for a rewarding state in the afterlife.

61

kasab yim k̡aran ta namāz guzāran
niz tim yath samsāras zāi
chhakh lāganai barith pānai karan
papith yiyakh baḍ rāhakai
tāra taran ta nāra ubaran
tavuk fāz[114] *diyakh pāna khudāy*

Those who engage in spiritual discipline
  and who offer prayers
    are truly born to this world.
They plant in abundance and nurture it.
On ripening, they have a big harvest.
They will go across and
  emerge from the fire.
God Himself will reward them for it.

62

zän myon chhuy amrĕta görō
tami ādur samsāra gava[115]
gav gŏras tsāṭha tsörō
tithuy me var dita diva

My Zaina churns the nectar—
  He renounced the world with honor.
The disciple surpassed his preceptor.
Bless me like that, God!

---

[114] reward, benefit, or bounty, Grierson, vol. II, p. 723.
[115] In the Saqi collection, this word in the verse (p. 150) appears as "kiva". The transcription in the Parimoo collection (v. 115) used here, however, makes more sense.

63

fikar chhuy dozakhas vurun[116] *thörō*[117]
fikar chhuy ambiyāhan hunduy khŏi
fikar chhuy alug ta palug[118] *tsörō*
fikar chhuy mushikh ta khŏshbŏi
fikras pĕṭh yus rūd dörō
tas chhuy yeti kyā tati öbrŏy

Contemplation is protection from hell.
Contemplation is the path of prophets.
Contemplation suffices for this world and the next.
Contemplation is the aroma and the fragrance.
He who is firmly established in contemplation
is honored both here and hereafter.

64

manas khai kās zan āyīnas
tava zanas gatshī zänī zān
thali thali kyā chhuy shuri mŏkha pānas
marnas brōnṭh mar suy chhuy gyān

Remove the rust from
your heart as if from a mirror.
That is how you will be
acquainted with Him.
So youthful is your face and body.
Die before your death[119]—
that is knowledge.

[116] to wrap oneself or cover onself; protection, Grierson, vol. II, p. 1142.
[117] from thar: fear; dozakhas tharo: the fear of hell, Grierson, vol. II, p. 982
[118] alug ta palug (iha-lōka ta para-lōka): this world and the hereafter.
[119] See Verses, n. 64.

65

namāzi parĕḥ ta pān thana vasī[120]
namāzi dŏdas khasī tar
namāzi ulag ta pulag[121] *lasī*
namāzi bihashtas[122] *vusī bar*

If you offer prayers, you will be reborn.
Praying will separate the cream from the milk.[123]
Praying will make you flourish in
this world and the hereafter.
Praying will open the door to the paradise.

66

'alim bŏḍ tai kälima sōvū
muhammad pälith vudi pakakh vatei
krei variyini mŏkhtay̆ lōdū
bāvücha dāvath su tath vatei

Knowledge is great,
so recite the sacred words.[124]
On following Muhammad,
you will walk on the path awake.
A year of good deeds,
a heap of pearls.
A feast of devotion—
He is on that path.

---

[120] thana vasun or thana pyon: to be born, Grierson, vol. II, pp. 977–78.
[121] ulag ta pulag or alug ta palug (iha-lōka ta para-lōka): See Verses, n. 118.
[122] paradise or heaven.
[123] The "cream" symbolizes the higher Self, which reveals itself through purification brought about by offering prayers on a regular basis.
[124] The reference here is to the benefit of reciting the "kalima" or the sacred formula in order to firmly establish it in the heart. See Verses, n. 49.

67

poz dapun chhuy nāra drāv sŏn zan
mūri aryan zan gāshur pĕyei
apuz dapun chhuy būta asun zan
yimna phäli vavizi ta tim kati bovei

Truth is like gold forged in fire.
Awakened beings are radiant.
Lies are like illusion.
Don't sow seeds that won't sprout.

68

subahaki vakta farishta vasan
groshen[125] *kŏsa chhava āsan shai*
zal yim chāvan ta mal yim kāsan
timan yĕti khŏta tati āsan shai

Angels will descend in the morning,
greeting those who are honorable.
Those who offer water to others and
those who remove impurities
will be honored there more than here.

---

[125] from grösherun: to receive, Grierson, vol. I, p. 305.

Reverence

69

kandi māji chhiva nyūl katrān
tranan divān drōtū
kona māji chhiva paluk[126] *sŏrān*
tati hōrun[127] *barun kötū*

Hey, ladies, you are cutting
  the grass with strikes from your sickle.
Why don't you remember the hereafter?
A lot would have to,be repaid there.

70

pöni varāh zāth na andī
kandi māji tsaṭakh sabzas gand
bahāruk sabzā ḍyūnṭh asi vandi
āsan shai chhai shahar and
lachhāh mārith kyāh dikh grandi[128]
gatsh prakatsh zānun kaḍith and

Without good deeds, no goodness is within.
You are destroying the fragrance of grass.
We dreamed of the spring greenery in the winter.
Reverence can be found only in the city outskirts.
After killing so many, what would be your reckoning?
Learn to remove your inborn instincts.[129]

---

[126] from paralōka: hereafter or the other world.
[127] to repay a debt, Grierson, vol. I, p. 349.
[128] reckoning, Grierson, vol. I, p. 303.
[129] This verse suggestively conveys that humans are born with the instinct to think of their own survival first before they think of the well-being of others. That instinct can be overcome by cultivating compassion for all living beings, including the non-human life in nature.

71

yod bōzakh shōtakh gŏrapandei
yī dīnshith reshi rūdi vanan and
khyōkhna bokh ohar[130] *ava prakth mondei*[131]
shabhath röst khyōkh vopalhāk ta hand[132]

Listen to the teacher's advice!
On witnessing such sights,
  Rishis retreated to backwoods.
They abstained from delicious food,
  so nature is not made dreary—
They ate flavorless wild greens and chicory.

72

yiha mäji zuv chhus ta kĕtha tsaṭize
zuvas zuv dizina zāth (zānh)
länis lekhitis kyāh karize
asi ha mäji vuchhav chon sandbhāv

It has life—why do you cut it?
Do not sacrifice life for nothing.
Nothing can be done about one's lot.
I just wanted to find out
  your true intention.[133]

---

130 bokh ohar: delicious food.
131 prakath: nature; mondei: to get blunt or dreary.
132 vopalhāk: wild green vegetable; hand: chicory.
133 The verses (69–72) are in the form of a dialogue with a group of women Nūruddīn comes across on his travels (Parimoo, pp. 270–76). The women are cutting the grass. As a response to Nūruddīn's question as to why they are cutting the grass, one of the women says that she is cutting it to feed her cow. In v. 72 Nūruddīn acknowledges that sometimes taking from nature cannot be avoided. He reveals that he had admonished the women because he wanted to see if they were mindlessly destroying nature or if they had a good reason to do so.

73

dāndas vandei[134] *phala gāsa pālanas*
sōnta raṭith ganḍanas maṭhō
bihei ta trōpith nāra lōv zālanas
huei karith tulanas muranas loṭū
pakinai ada tas tsak vāni lāganas
lāl za āvrith karanas goṭū
maka shrāki patō pōs ada vālanas
bram kandi barakh chhu samsār tshēṭū

A buffalo is raised on fodder.
In spring, he is tied to a plough.
If he sits, they burn a packed
sheaf of grass under him.
After saying "hui," they raise
and twist his tail.
If he can't walk, he is put to use
in the miller's shop.
Covering his eyes,
his world is made dark.
In the end, his skin is removed
with a sharp knife.
If you are attached to the body,
the world is tainted.

[134] from vandun: to offer, Grierson, vol. II, p. 1123.

74.

mīshas khash na karnas pazī
zān ta vuchh suy kapṭān[135]
yod myōn gŏr pad sezī[136]
akuy zuv baḍi buh gindān

It is not good to slaughter a sheep.
Recognize that only He apportions.
If you follow my teaching—
  only One Spirit plays in the big world.

75

kandĕv māriv mīn hā zuva shamīn
yim zuv mārith zuvas dīn
timay duniyahaki bramīn
Nakīr ta Munkīr javābas yīn
teli mĕll āsmān ta zamīn

Why do you kill fish
  to appease the self?
Those who kill living creatures
  to feed the living are
    the deluded of the world.
Nakir and Munkir will come to
  demand an answer when
    the earth and the sky meet.[137]

---

[135] to divide out in portions, Grierson, vol. I, p. 464.
[136] from sĕzrān: to aim straight at a mark, Grierson, vol. II, p. 959
[137] Nakir and Munkir are two angels who, according to Muslim belief, descend to the graveside of the dead to check their account of good and bad deeds.

Scholar

76

dänishmand chhuy amarĕt gorū
phyör phyör asĕs pashpān
brōnh kani hĕth āsi kitāba börū
vuchhith āsi ṭānjarān[138]
vuchhun hyöt chhu andara tshörū
paras pranith mashas pān

A learned man churns nectar.
A stream of drops trickles down his face.
A pile of books he has in front of him—
Consulting these, he acts passionate.
When we begin to see, he is empty inside.
He forgets himself while reproaching others.[139]

77

parān parān par gäi
tim khar gai kitāb bār hĕth
yim dila nish bākhabar gäi
tim nar gai fäzal[140] *ta ata (atha) hĕth*

Reading continuously, they are alienated.
They turn into donkeys with a load of books.
Those who are aware of the truth in the heart,
are blessed with grace.

---

[138] from ṭanz: extreme and urgent desire or passionate (to finish some work or the like), Grierson, vol. II, p. 1012.

[139] Nūruddīn critiques scholars whose knowledge of God is based on reading books and hence, on intellectual knowledge. In contrast, mystics' knowledge of God is based on the inner revelation in the heart. For scholars, he says, preaching is an occupation that allows them to make money, which they use to fulfill their desire for material things.

[140] from fäiz, a free gift or grace, Grierson, vol. I, p. 723.

78

aval paran ta pärith anan
khalkan nīkī kanan āsei
lari lädith tshünan asmānan
zānan duniyā suribŏn āsei
akhärath trävith māzan danan
so bŏd hājū[141] *hevānan āsei*

First they read, and then they preach.
For common people
goodness lies in listening.
They build houses that reach the sky
as if the world is a heap of ashes.
Ignoring the hereafter,
they care only for wealth.
Hey, animals have such thinking.

79

'alimuk bŏr lödahakh kharan
karan gŏnāh bandgī sahibsüi
hasada naphāka prakath[142] *baran*
tim havāla karikh shetānsai

The burden of knowledge is
piled up on donkeys.
They commit sins in the name of God.
Filled with hatred and inflated ego,
they have been put in charge of the devil.

---

[141] hā juva: respectful interjection for calling, Grierson, vol. I, p. 370.
[142] naphāka: bloated or inflated, Grierson, vol. I, p. 645; prakath: one's nature or one's ego.

80

'alim parith zōnukh asi gäi vĕṭhi
tim vĕṭhi gögal[143] *ṭĕṭhī*[144]*gäi*
yim mātam hĕth andvan bīṭhī
tim tal äsith pĕṭhī gäi

After acquiring knowledge,
they think they are great.
Those insolent fat ones
become conceited.
Those who retreat
into backwoods in sorrow,
in spite of their low position,
they rise high.

81

malō chhölukh ta malō chhökukh
malō ḍyunṭhmai na 'alimuk nāv
malō tati bŏna bartal ḍölukh
malō laz rāvaruth mala nāv

You have been cleansed by Mullahs and
you have been scattered by Mullahs.
Mullah, I don't see a trace of knowledge in you.
Mullah, you lost your way at the door.
Shame on you, Mullah—
you don't deserve to be called a Mullah.

143 arrogant or insolent, Grierson, vol. I, p. 279.
144 pretentious or conceited, Grierson, vol. II, p. 1041.

82

mala chhiva töhi ta manza kam dŏsa
tshalas chhiva zāgān akis akh
'alim chhiva parān māshiki[145] *hāvasa*[146]
mehmān ḍīshith yivān tsakh
yĕti chhuva gumāna asi chhi khāsa
tati no mŏkaliv sāsa manza akh

You are Mullahs—
  Why are you divided?
You are ready to cheat one another.
You aquire knowledge
  to fulfill your desires.[147]
You get angry on seeing a guest.
You are proud that you are the chosen ones.
Not one in a thousand amongst you will escape there.

83

malai āsi zi ti mŏlai romī
na ta karizi ruma ruma istifkār[148]
södaras tār dituy tamī
pānai sapun pānas yār

If there was a Mullah—it was Rumi.
Otherwise you should repent deeply.
He crossed the ocean and
  achieved self-realization.

---

[145] practice for aquiring, usage, Grierson, vol. 1, p. 362.
[146] havas or hāvas: eager desire or inordinate appetite, Grierson, vol. I, p. 597.
[147] The reference here is to the idea that scholars' real motivation to aquire knowlegde is to engage in a profession to fulfill their worldly desires unlike Rishī Sufis, who retreat into solitude to free themselves of desires in order to become perfect receptacles for divine knowledge.
[148] repentence.

84

'alim chhuy boḍ ta mala chhukh dānā
jabar yeti sanā kihō
ārarös ḍyūnṭhmakh tōrirös chhānā
varahöl arkhali zina[149] *hihō*
asi yeti rachāv dayi sund panāh
fakīra kava goy kānā hihō
undas kalima chhuy dayi sund panāh
mĕvarös ḍyūnṭhmak vanā hihō
sahĕb pānai yeti ladi khānā
pāna khŏta byākh zān dānā hihō

You have great knowledge
  and you are a wise Mullah.
Where there is coercion,
  no gratitude is there.
I see you without compassion like
  a carpenter without an adze—
You are like the twisted arkhol[150] wood.
We sought here God's refuge—
  why do you take an ascetic for a begger?
The sacred words[151] are God's refuge within—
  I see you as a fruitless forest.
Lord himself will build a house here.
Rather than yourself,
  consider the other as wise.

[149] The original word in the Saqi collection is "gina," but it seems to be incorrect as "zina" or "zyun" fits the context.
[150] See Verses, n. 36.
[151] See Verses, n. 49.

Advice

85

nafas algun[152] *chhuy achh manz siryun*
gāshich vŏmed barizi na zāt (zānh)
nafas algun chhuy āra manzi yirun
halis[153] *ta mĕndis*[154] *garai vāt*

Gratifying the ego is like
creating a mirage—
never hope for enlightenment.
Gratifying the ego is like
floating downsteam—
you will arrive at the dwelling
of the crooked and the deformed.

86

su gul kyā mangi gulas ta gulistānas
yas ṭäṭhis jānas chhāngar gayei
su kyā mangi āftābakis nūrānas
yas andmädānas nĕndar pĕyei

A flower whose dear life is destroyed
can ask for nothing from
the flower or the garden.
He who falls asleep in a secluded place
can ask for nothing from
the bright light of the sun.

---

152 to gratify.
153 from höl: crooked.
154 someone who is wasted away by disease or ill health.

87

su chhuna vuchhān qīlas ta qālas[155]
su chhuy vuchhān dila kis hālas[156] *kun*
zikri haq par zĕv dith tālas
rāzahonz yiyī zālas kun

He does not judge you
  by your arguments.
He judges you by your spiritual state.
Remember God with
  the tongue stuck to the palate.[157]
So the royal swan[158] is drawn to your net.

88

kānan tihandĕn därizina sipar
kartaj chhŏkan phirizĕs na rŏy
balāyi tahänzei vĕndizĕkh[159]*shakar*[160]
ada chhuy yeti kyā tati ōbrŏy[161]

Block not His arrows with a shield.
Turn not your face away
  from His sword thrusts.[162]
Consider calamities from Him as blessing.
You receive honor then
  both here and hereafter.

---

155 intellectual arguments.
156 spiritual state.
157 a spiritual practice that involves the control of breath, which is accompanied by the recitation of God's name.
158 The royal swan refers to the Beloved in Sufi terminology.
159 from vĕndun: to consider, Grierson, vol. II, p. 1125.
160 sugar; metaphorical meaning: blessing.
161 from abrū: honor.
162 This verse suggests that suffering itself can teach seekers and give them the strength to move forward on the spiritual path.

89

zĕth pĕth ta basta dajī
mīlith boh ta mŏlaji chhei[163]
sva yemi gaṇḍ tas olūd tsajī
äkharatas käts tas phratsī[164] *chhei*
dil yemi gönḍ ta prakath tsajī
tas dargāh vath mŏkajī chhei

After birth, the body
joined with "I" becomes precious.
He who controls the body,
his impurities are removed.
In the end, it becomes auspicious.
He who controls the mind, purifies his nature.
For him, the door to the inner sanctuary is open.

90

nafasai man matsrāvī
mĕṭhi ta zĕṭhi[165] *putshei*[166]
tavay ulag ta pulag rāvī
kuni nata kava māl putshei

The lower self causes craving
for the delicious and the elegant.
You thus lose this world and the hereafter—
for whom and to what end, my dear.

---

[163] In the Saqi collection, the first two lines of Verse 339 are given as "zaṭ paṭ ta basta daji/meli ta buthi mŏlji chhai." Parimoo's transcription (v. 47, p. 61) of the lines used here seems more correct.

[164] Saqi's transcription (v. 339) of this word is 'phraji,' but Parimoo's transcription used here makes more sense.

[165] mĕṭhi ta zĕṭhi: the delicious and the elegant.

[166] from putshy: for, Grierson, vol. II, p. 808.

91

zaf kar yuth taph[167] *tsaranai*
yeli bokhta ohar haranai yin
shūb[168] *āsi lūb ta tsakh maranai*
yeli rish ta kibr[169] *zarnaiyi*[170] *na*
phal bovi kal trāyith kām karanai
ada tim tshari bāna baranai yin

Remember God and practice austerities.
When your appetite for food is lost,
  you will become graceful.
Your greed and anger will die
  and hate and pride will not last.
Performing actions with detachment will bear fruit.
Only then empty vessels will be filled to the brim.

92

zadĕn[171] *manz lāl mo khōlan*[172]
zālan manz jānvār bōlan mo
sura ladĕn yembarzala mo phŏlan
kātsa vānan mŏkhtahār melan mo

Stagnant water does not contain pearls.
Trapped birds do not sing.
Daffodils do not bloom in heaps of ashes.
Pearl necklaces are not found
  in glass-blowers' shops.

---

[167] austerities.
[168] shūb: spledour, elegance, grace, Grierson, vol. II, p. 869.
[169] rish: hate; kibr: pride.
[170] from zarun or zarawun: to endure, Grierson, vol. II, p. 1232–33.
[171] from zaḍ: motionless, Grierson, vol. II, 1216.
[172] from khōlu: void, having nothing of, Grierson, vol. I, p. 398.

93

zādei pōsh dyolū avazātō
khĕyas na gur gupan ta gāv
su yeli shahas sheri vōtū
su avazātū drinṭh[173] *kati āv*

Of inferior variety is
the stem of marsh flower[174]—
the horse and the cattle don't eat it.
In a wreath when it reaches the king's head,
no longer is it seen as inferior.

94

riziq chhuy brōnṭh ta mōt chhuy pata
dunyā chhu shahruk ataigath[175]
sŏrun bugī ta gārus vata
bōzkhai chhai rozan neka bad kath

Sustenance comes first
and then death.
The world is like the coming
and going in a city.
Remember God and seek His path.
Listen, if you will—
good and bad deeds endure.

---

[173] from drish (Skt.): to be seen or viewed.

[174] The soft stem of marsh grass was used in medieval Kashmir for making twine to bind things together.

[175] coming and going; metaphoric meaning: birth and death, Grierson, vol. I, p. 54.

95

räni man rāzapŏrush anei
pakān ta āsmān man ladith[176]
tul boḍai sūrukh māl murādanei
yeli qabri sheri gatshanakh kani ladith

The king and the queen are blind—
they walk in full majesty.
They receive the most expensive
of what they desire
until the headstone is laid
on their decorated grave.

96

marg[177] *chhuy süh ṭa kötū tsalizei*
kheli manz kaḍī tsärith kaṭh
maragach sharbath chanaros na balizei
suli kĕth ta gayās märith kath

Death is a tiger—
you cannot escape it.
He will pick you out
like a sheep from a flock.
Without the elixir of death,[178]
you will not be cured.
How did I die early?[179]

---

[176] the literal meaning of this line is "they walk with their mind up in the sky".
[177] death, Grierson, vol. I, p. 590.
[178] This verse suggests the finality of death. No one can stop it and hence, the fear of death is deeply ingrained in human consciousness, more so in those who have no spiritual awakening. A seeker who has renouned the attachment to the worldly life or, in other words, "drank the elixir of death" is not afraid of death.
[179] The reference here is to Nūruddīn's renunciation of the world around the age of thirty.

97

ādama ganda mari nādānō
zagath börnai ṭōṭh
marakh ta ninai vadānō
kentsan path ta kentsan brōnṭh

Fool, an impure man dies.
He filled you with worldly love.
On death, they will carry you weeping
before some and after others.

98

yiman kyā karakh dyāran
yim hō rōzan yetī
namāzi putshi hō māran
pāph zīnith kütī
nazrā karto and mazāran
särī za tsamav tatī

What will you do with this wealth?
It will remain here.
Neglecting prayers will result in suffering.
Many bad deeds have you accumulated.
Keep in mind the graveyard at the end.
All of us will shrivel there.

99

yus ōra yamun bār vasī
tasei sōr 'ālam vadi ta lasi mō
yus ḍāyan gazan tal tubli vasī
suai nabī ti āsī khasi mō

On whomsoever descends
the angel of death,
he won't live even if
the whole world weeps.
One who is buried under
two and a half yards of earth,
he won't rise even if he were a prophet.

100

khānan handĕn yiman rōbakhānan
jānan dapān zi oorihund gatsh
sŏndari ḍesham huri vakhnāvān
tsamarav sütī ḍuvān latsh
tati az ḍīnṭhim kapasi khanān
nasra mĕ vuchh tsa vuchhni gatsh

In the harems of the khans, where
the good people are sent the other way,
I saw beautiful women singing songs
and removing dust with yakhair dusters.
Today I saw them there hoeing to plant cotton.
Nasr, I saw it—now you go and see.[180]

---

[180] The verse suggestively conveys the transitoriness of life. Money, glory, and enjoyment do not last.

101

kŏl mo lagī rangan ta sangan
kŏl mo hangan lekhanei āv
kŏl mo ashud lagī angan
daran 'amal[181] *nata kŏl kati āv*

Caste is of no use in fancy gatherings.
Caste is not written on one's face.
Caste won't make your body parts impure.
If you perform your duties—
there is no caste.

102

dŏd trävith yus tshör pōni mandei
suy samsāras kandei zāv
ohar karahāv hākas ta handei
andvan nīrith tapasī hāv
par ta pān yus hihuy vĕndei
suy bŏhsĕndei tarith drāv

Renouncing milk who churns only water,
he is the one born to the world.[182]
We ought to eat leafy greens and chicory
and go into the backwoods for penance.
He who considers himself and the other as the same,
he is the one who crosses the worldly river.

---

181 from darun: to perform a fast or other religious obligation, Grierson, vol. I, p. 246; amal: action.

182 The word "water" symbolizes the material world and "milk" the divine reality. If one is preoccupied with improving one's lot in the material world to the neglect of the divine reality, one belongs fully to this world and hence, physical death is the end of one's life. However, through spiritual discipline a person can seek for one's birth along another axis of consciousness and hence, lessen the hold of physical death as one can traverse two worlds simultaneously.

103

vĕdei mĕtra byoluy vavizei
saga kani dizĕs haṭi kuy rath[183]
yārnai ḍeshihan kyā karizei
yār kati travei yār sänz kath

Knowingly sow the seeds of friendship.
Sacrifice your very life to nurture them.
What will you do if you don't see the Friend?
The Friend will never abandon a friend.

104

tsök ta mödur ṭyöth ta zahar
khūni jigar[184] *yemi öhar khĕv*
yemi yöt pĕṭh hets tśĕd ta kahar
su tath shahar gatshith pĕv

Sweet and sour,
bitter and poisonous.
He who survives a bleeding heart
and who patiently suffers,
he goes to that city and stays there.

---

[183] haṭi kuy rath: literal meaning, the blood of one's throat; metaphorical meaning, to give up one's life or to sacrifice one's life.
[184] khūni jigar: bleeding heart.

105

krei māntan chila darun
kamas na daran nafas duvandei
zahar khěth yim ādaran
tim öhar karan hākas ta handei
sonta tim jakhan lāgnay karan
tim sŏkh baran papi vandei
yim na khudāy ta rasūl saran
tim samsāras zěn ta kandei

Consider going on a retreat a good deed.
Ascetics are not afraid of consuming less.
They become humble from eating little.
They live on leafy greens and chicory,
  arduously cultivating the land in spring—
    they rejoice in the harvest season.[185]
Those who do not remember God and the Prophet,
  they are born to the world as body.

106

akis bartal sāzanda vāyān
vud chhu lägith něndrei hotū
běyis razi ta lorei lāyān
pāna āshan kas kyā dyutū

At someone's door musicians play—
  Though awake, he pretends to be drowsy.
Another is beaten with a whip and a stick.
God himself distributes.

---

[185] See Verses, n. 113.

107

nāvi vasakh gāh wŏkhali khasakh[186]
dutsyöt karna basakh mō vai
yödavai aki vati mahkam āsakh
dūr panthana lōsakh mō vai
yām na dunyihiki zanzīr kāsakh
tām zŏsakh ta āsakh mō vai

Sometimes you get into the boat
and sometimes you walk on foot.
In two minds, alas, you won't survive.
If you follow one path firmly,
far away destinations
will not make you weary.
Until you break the chains of this world,
you won't be content.

108

kentsan roza ta namāza zimei
timan bugī rūd pāna hyötū
kentsan vumbar sar gayi lamei[187]
pana āshan kas kyā dyutū

To some is given the responsibility
of fasting and praying.
To them God Himself is benevolent.
Some waste their life completely—
God himself distributes.

---

[186] to walk on foot.

[187] "vumbar gayi lamai" comes from the idiom "vans lama gatshan" which means to waste one's life.

109

nār gatshi sahun[188] *ta āra gatshi gālun*
öhar gatshi karun vopalhākas ta handei
had[189] *gatshi raṭun ta mad gatshi vālun*
veh gatshi tsālun ta tava atsi zagarnandei
shŏb gatshi kānchhun ta lūb gatshi mārun
pān gatshi tārun buhsĕndei

Accept hardships and let go of self-pity,
subsist on wild greens and chicory,
practice moderation and renounce pride,
endure sorrow—then you will experience bliss.
Aspire for goodness and renounce greed.
Make the self go across the worldly river.

110

nafasas mo daph badal
nafasas sūtī sodā chhuy
nafasai panun raṭun hadai
nafasai prazanith[190] *khŏdā chhuy*

Don't abuse the lower self—
strike a bargain with the lower self
Keep your ego under control.
On recognizing the lower self,
God is attained.[191]

---

[188] literal meaning: to "endure the fire." The fire here stands for hardship.
[189] had raṭun: to limit or to practice moderation.
[190] from prazanāvun: to recognize.
[191] The reference here is to the first stage in the spiritual journey that involves recognizing the reality of the lower self and disciplining the ego and its preoccupation with fulfilling material desires.

111

gŏra kath chhei nābad ta ṭang
yöd rōtsī[192] *ta prayī*
gatshith gōr gŏras mang
tava vondas shihlith pĕyī
tavai tsalī rōzun bang[193]
khudā ti atha yiyī

The preceptor's teaching
is candy and pears
if you accept it and love it.
Visit your preceptor and
ask for his blessings
so your heart calms down.
Your confusion will go away—
You will find God only then.

112

kentsan dituth yeti kyā va tötuy
kentsan yeti na ta tötuy kyāh
kentsan dituth lāluk tröṭuy[194]
kentsan gāshi manz göṭai gāh

To some you gave both here and there.
Others received nothing here or there.
To some you gave a necklace of gems.
Others experienced darkness in the midst of light.

---

192 to be agreeable.
193 confusion.
194 See Verses, n. 111.

113

kentsan dyutukh torai ālav[195]
kentsav rachāyi nālai[196] *vĕth*
kentsan mas cheth achh laji tālav[197]
kentsan nyūluy tsäli hālav[198] *khĕth*
kenh gäli mūla ta kenh gäli mālav
kents gäi vānan phālav dith[199]

Some received the divine call.
Others put in extreme effort
  for divine grace.
Some drank the divine wine
  and were intoxicated.
Others lost their unripe crop
  to the locusts.
Some were wiped away
  due to destitution.
Others were lost due to possessions.
Some abandoned their shops.[200]

---

[195] torai ālav dyun: literal meaning, getting a call from the other side or a divine call; metaphoric meaning, effortless progress in spiritual attainment.
[196] nāla raṭun: to seize by the neck or to seize forcibly; vĕth: Jehlum river. The idomatic meaning in this context is to put in extreme effort to receive divine grace.
[197] ächhi laji tālav: literal meaning, eyes glued to the ceiling; metaphoric meaning, divine intoxication.
[198] hālav: locusts, A related idiom is: "papith gay hālav khĕth," which means a soon-to-finish work is unexpectedly destroyed. The usage in the above verse implies that sometimes people work hard at planting and nurturing the seeds of good thoughts and deeds, but they are led astray due to unexpected outside events over which they have no control.
[199] phālav dyun: to shut down.
[200] Nūruddīn compares the spiritual journey to planting a crop, nurturing it, and then harvesting it. The harvested crop turns the farmer into a trader. Similarly, steady progress on the path turns the aspirant into a trader with accumulated merit to be exchanged in the hereafter. The buyer in this analogy is God. The last line refers to those people who accumulate good deeds, but then lose interest and turn their attention to something else.

114

nafas chhuy vanuk agazolū[201]
nerĕs na paṭ kūṭ[202] *manzalū*
yemi tsöṭ anith gaji zōlū
tamī sharai muhammad pōlū

The ego is the knotted wood of the forest—
not good enough for
making the frame of a cradle.
He who chops it down, brings it home,
and burns it in the kitchen fire,
he follows the path of Muhammad.

115

āsi chhänis ṭĕnṭh ta baritas gŏbĕr
āsi tota köl ta kāvas gänṭh[203]
āsi nihāl trödith phalchi gŏbĕr
āsi päz[204] *vanan ta pāthli*[205] *gänṭh*

The empty one shows off
and the full one is sober.
The parrot does not speak
and the crow turns into an eagle.
The prosperous is grounded
by the weight of his possessions.
The falcon is in the forest
and the eagle in the plains.

---

[201] aga: knot in a tree, Grierson, vol. I, p. 16; zolū: an interstice or a network, Grierson, vol. II, p. 1221.
[202] frame.
[203] eagle or a vulture.
[204] a falcon or a hawk, Grierson, vol. II, p. 819.
[205] a low plain at the foot of a mountain.

116

aval suy äkhar suy
nadabal vasith mal käsiv
das guli gandith tas kun äsiv
děv kuni dōzakhani nār lasiv

He is the first and the last.
Go down the river bank
and remove your impurities.
Fold your hands and turn towards Him.
Perhaps you will be saved from the fire of hell.

117

raṭus pāntsh nadazala[206] *vuhan*[207]
huhun nīla pavan dith khan
suy pav madai sandārun[208]
tava ti něri hyōt[209] *anman*[210]

Control the flow of the five rivers[211]—
breathe in deeply.[212]
Use the same breath to control your pride.
It will lead to valuable knowledge.

---

206 pāntsh nadazala: the five rivers symbolizing the five sense organs.

207 from vahun: flow, Grierson, vol. II, 1104.

208 to put in order or to control, Grierson, vol. II, p. 920.

209 hyōt něrun: to become beneficial, Grierson, vol. I, p. 367.

210 ability to understand or comprehend the purpose of one's work, Grierson, vol. I, 34.

211 The reference here is to the need to control the five sense organs, which bring in sense impressions without interruption and lead to a distracted state of mind.

212 In various esoteric traditions, breathing techniques are used to control the mind and direct one's attention inwards.

118

chhi päzan āprān ta kŏkar tachhān[213]
chhi muḍan pherān bartal trukī
chhi sŏzan jakhān kŏzan khĕvān
chhi zäkir[214] *härān gäfal sökhī*

The immature are fed
  and the mature are in distress.
At the door of the ignorant,
  the wise are turned away.
The good toil and the wicked devour.
The devout are bewildered
  and the ignorant are happy.

119

kentsan qabar chhei pōsh zan sherei
kentsan qabar chhei siyāh chāh
kenh gäli sahĕba sanzei vīrei
kenh gaiei zerei aki gumrāh

To some the grave is a bed of flowers.
To others the grave is a dark abyss.
Some languish away for the Lord.
Some lose their way by just one push.

---

[213] the literal meaning of this line is: "The chicks are fed and the chicken scratch."
[214] from zäkir: one who remembers God.

120

lālach qadar ḍūngal zānei
pösh kyā zānei söthi pĕṭhi vath[215]
shamaich qadar lash kyā zānei
machh kyā zānei pömpari gath

A diver knows the worth of pearls.
An animal knows not
the value of the straight path.
A torch knows not the value of flame.
A fly knows not a moth's fate.

121

andvan nīrith tap tsarhāv[216]
öhar karahāv vopalhākas ta handei
āmtsai tsakh yöd path karahāv
tī yöd karahāv marhāv kandei

Retreating into the backwoods,
engaging in austerities,
subsisting on bitter greens and chicory
and letting go of the inner anger—
from practicing that,
we would die to the body.

[215] söthi pĕṭh vath: literal meaning, path along the embankment; metaphoric meaning, straight path.
[216] from tap charya: performing penance.

122

kandi pānas mō di randei[217]
ami sābani sāfī na athei
ami tasbīh 'āsa ta jandai
ami fandai su yiyi no athei
kal trävith ās māli bandai
athi tava yiyi akai kathei[218]
na ta tati āsakh sharmandai
sahĕb akuy yeti kyā tatei
döl trävith[219] *lāg charan dai*
höl mo pakh pakhtō vatei
pantsan yandan yus diyi nĕndai[220]
tami ḍyūnṭh vonda ada suy matei

Don't rub your body—
  the soap will not clean it.
The rosary, staff and the patched robe—
  these tricks will not lead you to Him.
Renounce desires, my dear,
  and become a servant.
Only then will you grasp the real teaching.
Ashamed you will be there otherwise.
The same Lord is both here and there.
Supplicate and seek refuge.
Walk on the right path
  and not on the crooked one.
He who purifies five sense organs,
  sees in the heart and is ecstatic.

---

[217] randa dyun: to make smooth, over and over, Grierson, vol. II, p. 836.
[218] akai kath: the real or true teaching.
[219] döl travith (idiom): spreading the skirt to supplicate.
[220] literal meaning: to remove weeds; metaphoric meaning: to purify.

123

tandarustī chhei nyāmatsa sāsā
gāsū phirāsā[221] *shukar kar*
krei kāran sŏkhan olāsa[222]
tagiyei rāth dĕn khudāy sar
garībī chhay khās-al-khāsā
kharīdār chhuy khudā sōdā kar
duniyādārī bukari sāsā
tavāl ta andakār[223] *mō tsa bar*

A thousand blessings is good health—
Be thankful for your mortal body.
Good deeds are the means
  of enjoying happiness.
Remember God day and night, if you can.
Poverty is the best of the best.
God is the buyer, strike a bargain.
Worldliness has a thousand faces.
Add not to the delay and darkness.

---

[221] gāsu phirāsa: mortal body.
[222] from ullāsa: enjoyment.
[223] tavāl ta andakār: delay and darkness.

124

ada na yi kạrakh ti ada na tagī
ādana karakh ta lagī sütī
yim phali vavakh chhati kyā zagī
tim tati äkhartas lōnakh kütī
giha bal trävith diha bal lagīy
ada nund ta ḍūṭh lagī pānas sütī

If you don't do something,
you won't learn it.
What you do in youth will stay with you.
Whatever seeds you sow—white or brown,
you will reap there in the end.
Renouncing your attachment to home
will make your body strong.
The good and the bad then will stay with you.

125

'āsa ta divur chhuy jörmutuy
räshi ta bŏgza chhuy börmut pān
duhali bata[224] *chhuy hörmutuy*[225]
kava zāna atha kati lagī īmān

Your staff and your whip are engraved.
You are filled with hatred and jealousy.
Your daily subsistence is from others.
How can you develop honesty?

---

[224] duhali bata: daily subsistence.
[225] owing to others.

126

sat srānas phal yöd pōshihei
gāḍi ta krämas[226] *äs akay zāt*
vopas[227] *dinai dai yöd toshihei*
drälid[228] *leli*[229] *vai*[230] *tshinähei ṇa zāt (zānh)*

If seven baths were enough
to bear any fruit, the nature
of the fish and the crocodile
would be the same.
If God were happy without austerities,
the destitute would never put rice in the pot.

127

andara krūd trāvakh nata
nĕbra krūl kandei[231]
anta mal kāsakh na ta
chhöni votha beṭh kandei

If you don't let go
of the inner anger,
it will manifest in your actions.
If you don't get rid of
the inner impurities,
your actions are empty.

---

[226] crocodile.
[227] austerities.
[228] poor, needy or destitute, Grierson, vol. I, p. 243.
[229] pot.
[230] rice.
[231] The literal meaning of this line is: "you will develop sores on the outside."

128

parān parān pālun möṭhum
lekhān lekhān zōlum dil
zikri sütī khudāy ṭūṭhum
fikri sütī röchhum shil

Reading continuously, I forgot to follow.
Writing continuously, I burned my heart.
Through recitation, I became endeared to God.
Through reflection, I protected my virtue.

129

zuva kandi vuchhāmei kraha[232] *zan*
jangla khah[233] *zai pyeyei*
ādana lōgtham rahzan
yi rahzan manai chhuyei
bugi yitha vĕndizihan sahzan[234]
tathi shāh zan āsahakh sheyei

O body, I see you as if from a distance.
From the forest you seem to have
slipped into a cultivated field.
You acted like a robber in youth—
the robber is the mind.
If you had devoted yourself to God truthfully,
you would then have been the king of the six.[235]

---

[232] from kruh: a certain measure of distance, Grierson, vol. I, p. 469.
[233] a cultivated field, Grierson, vol. I, p. 394.
[234] truthfully or sincerely.
[235] The "six" stands for the mind and five sense organs. The reference here is to the idea that if one is devoted to God, it is easy to control the mind and the five sense organs.

130

sarĕn jāyei chhei and mazāran
käli yāran sŏhbath rāvei
sang chhai vänij duniyādāran
māzan dyāran pulag[236] *rāvei*
niz tim yim zi khudāy gāran
samith pūrā taran ḍavei

Everyone's place in the end
  is in the graveyard.
In time we lose the company of our friends.
Worldly people are stone-hearted—
  from desiring wealth,
    they lose the other world.
Those who search for God truthfully—
  completely focused,
    they race across the river.

131

kyā kari dandarös ḍūnis
kyā kari ranis tīr kamān
kyā kari mŏkhta hār hūnis
kyā kari anis padmān[237]

A toothless man cannot break a walnut.
A cripple has no use for a bow and arrow.
A pearl necklace is of no use to a dog.
A blind man appreciates not a beautiful woman.

---

236 pulag (par-lōka): the other world or the hereafter.
237 beautiful woman, Grierson, vol. I, p. 682.

132

süh tsāy gŏphan ta shāl chhi grazān
gäyi mandōri hani pyĕv nanzan gāsh
gadā[238] *gäy gänī*[239] *ta muhim pĕv rāzan*
händi bīṭhi nayan[240] *gov vāzan khash*[241]

As tigers retreat into caves,
jackals howl.
As the big house crumbles,
the little houses are illuminated.
As the poor flock together,
kings are troubled.
As the sheep sit in the open, cooks suffer.

133

gänṭh kyā zāni āyari vasun[242]
mänath[243] *kyā zāni mödur dāth*[244]
shānt kyā zāni lalanai rasun[245]
hänṭh kyā zāni prasun kyāt

An eagle knows how to go after the prey.
A healer knows not a sweet medicine.
A calm person knows how to cradle a child.
A barren woman knows not how to deliver a baby.

---

[238] a mendicant or a beggar, Grierson, vol. I, p. 276.
[239] to become dense or to flock, troop, Grierson, vol. I, p. 287.
[240] in the open.
[241] literal meaning: slaughtered; metaphorical meaning: suffered.
[242] āyari vasun: going after the prey.
[243] healer.
[244] medicine.
[245] lalanai rasun: cradle a baby.

134

handis pökhur ladizi ta hĕyi mō
bahari hanz āyir karimō tshīntsh
tāpan pōni thavizi ta zĕyi mō
muḍas pranizi ta hĕyi mo hītsh

The ram cannot bear
the burden of the plough.
The falcon cannot hunt like a hawk.
Water left out in the sun does not curdle.
A fool cannot learn words of wisdom.

135

hazrat bāba ādam mōlū
māma havā tatī āvo
ada kati vopun ḍūmb, vātal, tsrōlū[246]
kŏlas ham kŏl kyā heḍivū[247]

Adam was the father
Mother Eve followed him.
Where did lower castes come from?
How can members of the same family
ridicule one another?[248]

---

[246] ḍūmb, vātul, and tsrōl are the names of lower castes in medieval Kashmir.
[247] In the Saqi collection (p. 206) this word is transcribed as "herivū." The transcription in the Parimoo collection (v. 168, p. 155) used here makes more sense.
[248] Nūruddīn was against any caste system. In this verse, he refers to the story of Adam and Eve in order to convey to people that we all have descended from the same primeval Father and Mother and hence, we should not discriminate between people on the basis of caste, which was strictly observed by Hindus in medieval Kashmir.

136

anga yas khŏshbŏy mŏkha zan vudei
nishi vudĕn baḍ gath hĕth[249] *āsi mān*
sŏstai krei ta röstuy krūdei
suyei dapizei musalmān

He who has fragrant limbs
and an awakened face,
visits with reverence the spiritually awakened
and is honored there,
he who engages in good deeds
and is without anger—
he should be called a Muslim.

137

suy pŏrshāh sŏrgas prāvei
yas ahar chhuy beyan sān[250]
rātan dŏhan yus roza thāvei
āsi yava vasith navi namān
krūd lūb mad ahankār trāvei
suyei dapizei musalmān

That man reaches heaven
who is God-fearing,
fasts on holy days,
bows down with a pure mind,
renounces anger, greed, and pride—
he should be called a Muslim.

[249] baḍ gath hĕth: with great reverence.
[250] ahar chhuy beyan sān: God-fearing among others.

138

pānas mŏl karina hārei
süti bĕyis karina mānas mān
dŏrzan trävith sŏzan gārei
rātas dŏhas dāre dyān
par ta pān yus södaras tārei
suyei dapizei musalmān

He who values himself not a penny,
does not compete with others,
renounces the company of the wicked,
seeks out that of the good, prays day and night,
takes himself and others across the ocean—
he should be called a Muslim.

139

äkis mälis māji hündĕn
timan düy thävüth kyāi
musulmānan kyā va hendĕn
kar bandan tōshi khudāy

Born from a single
Father and Mother—
Do not discriminate
between Muslims and Hindus.
May God be pleased with his servants!

140

andvan nīrith pand yemi hetsei
satsei lōgun panun jān
yemi yaḍ ganḍ ta tsĕḍ tami hetsei
metsei vyöndun panun pān
andkun rahith bari yemi phetsei[251]
suyei dapizei musalmān

On retreating into the backwoods,
he who accepts suffering,
devotes himself totally to truth,
controls his appetite and is patient,
considers himself as nothing,
reflects on his heedlessness in solitude—
he should be called a Muslim.

141

tati kyā karav tshaṭi ta gaṭei
yeti lōlani välinj phaṭei hō
khabri rös qabar pāna raṭi nālumatei
māran kūntsh tati raṭei mō

What will we do in
the harsh wind and darkness there
where the desolate heart explodes?
The grave will embrace us
without any warning.
A lot of torment—
nobody to protect us there.

[251] heedlessness or forgetfuless, Grierson, vol. II, p. 719.

142

faqar yas vöndas shröpū
su zahmath tasänz rahmat vandei
tas kāluk nyūl ta pagahuk pöpū
suy gatshi tarith buha sĕndei
yimav khudāy ta rasool sörū
tī yemi pōl su tsāv grandei[252]

He whose heart is permeated with asceticism
 considers hardships as His mercy.
The unripe in his past and the future ripens.[253]
He who remembers God and the Messenger
 crosses the worldly river—
He who follows that path is the chosen one.

143

andara yas khabar vätsei ruhas
tas dōzakha tala käsĕkh tharei
yemi ḍanḍa kunḍa[254] *böchhī nĕndri ta muhas*
suy band tsāv sahas harei

He whose soul receives
 the revelation within,
  purged is he of the shivers of hell.
He who controls hunger,
 sleep, and attachment—
  that servant enters the company of the Lord.

---

252 grande atsun: to become the chosen one.

253 The reference here is to the idea that the still unripe seeds of good thoughts and actions will begin to grow and ripen with the proper spiritual practice.

254 ḍanḍa kunḍa: to control.

144

tōba yöd karakh bavasara tarakh
tōba chhuy vunikĕn tārvun nāv
tōba ros pāno tati kähi ubrakh
yeti chhai türi ta bushun vāv

If you repent, you will cross the worldly river.
Repentance is the ferry boat at this time.
Hey, self, without repentance
  how will you ascend there?
Here it is cold and no warmth.

145

anda kam vuchan banda kam āsan
qayāmüts[255] *ahvāl hai kyā āsei*
tāra kam taran nāra kam lasan
rahmata bartĕn hĕmathā āsei
dozakhun bayi chhu 'āmaṇ ta khāsan
qayāmüts tāmath suy hō āsei

Who identifies the blessed ones in the end?
What is the condition at the resurrection?
Who goes across and who remains unscathed by the fire?
Those filled with mercy will have courage.
The fear of hell is for both the common and the chosen.
Until the resurrection, He is the only one.

[255] The resurrection or the day of judgment, according to Muslim belief, will lead to the annihilation of the entire material world and all creatures, to the resurrection of the body, and the judgement of all beings for the life lived in this world. The righteous ones will go to heaven and the unrighteous ones to hell.

146

dyāran puran dāran ta ḍaban
yīts mō duniyihach kāman bar
ranj kar yi chhuy na kasbuk[256] *sāman*[257]
bugī subahan ta shāman sar
khotsan chhukh nō tōrachan pāman
atĕn gatshī dāman tar[258]

Wealth, a plot of land, doors and balconies—
don't desire the world so much.
Repent—these are not the means
of spiritual development.
Remember God morning and night.
Be afraid of the reproaches from the other world,
so you do not engage in bad deeds.

147

zikri sütī raṭun mālei
fikri sütī tārus pan
nafas ganḍ māli hālei hālei
zan tōruth mŏkhta mālei pan

Catch Him with remembrance, my dear.
Thread Him with reflection.
My dear, control your lower self little by little
as if you are threading a pearl necklace.

---

[256] craft or spiritual development.

[257] from sām: the staircase or ladder on the bank of a river for the convernience of the bathers, Grierson, vol. II, p. 910. The reference here is to the steps that the traveler on ṭhe path must traverse to make progress.

[258] dāman tar gatshun (literal meaning: soiling the hem of the robe) is an idiom, which means "to engage in sinful deeds or activities."

148

yemi asi bugi duniyahas sūzī
tas asi tōluq patshi[259] *lagav*
khasni ditin tŏrag ta täzī
timan khasith gäz[260] *karav*
tas path marav soray sōzī
yas asiy nam ta māz[261] *lagav*

God sent us to this world.
Through faith we establish
a relationship with Him.
Horses with whips he gave us to mount.[262]
We ride them and bring them under control.
If we die for Him, He will send to us everything.
He is near and dear to us.

149

allāh parnas dorā phirzei
zagatich lādan sarizina zānh
yādas tihändis dŏh dĕn barizei
zindai äsith marizi na zānh

Recite God's name constantly.
Don't be absorbed in worldly things.
Remember Him throughout the day.
Being alive, do not die.

---

259 Saqi's transcription (v. 149) is "putshi," whereas Afaqi's transcription "patshi" (vol. I, p. 529) used here makes more sense; patshi: faith, Grierson, vol. II, p. 807.

260 from gōzu: threatening, menace or reproof, Grierson, vol. I, p. 318.

261 nam ta māz lagav: just as nails are glued to the flesh, so is the divine intertwined with the human.

262 In medieval times, the term "horse" was used to refer to the body and the "whip" to the mind. The purpose of the spiritual discipline is to tame the body through disciplining the mind.

150

bulbul pōshi-vāri gārān
mogul gārān huni-vās
sūh shāl shuni-lay gārān
khar tshārān guhiled ta sās

The bulbul roams in a garden.
The owl wanders in empty dwellings.
The lion and the jackal roam in the wilderness.
A donkey sifts through dung and dirt.

151

yām chhuy tāpith dŏh garei
tām kämāh karto darketh
arzut kar[263] *mrata garei,*[264]
lūkan süti har khĕth
sömbarith mānchh thāvān tularei
patav gatshān tsarei khĕth

So long as the sun shines on you,
  engage in actions with enduring value.
Earn for the hour of your death.
Share your meals with others.
Bees collect honey in their hives
  and sparrows end up eating it.

---

[263] arzut kar: to earn wages.
[264] mrata garei: the hour of death.

Bibliography

Abu'l-Fazl. *'Ā'in-i-Akbarī* (1602). Trans. H. Blochmann. 1927. Lahore: Qausain, 1975.

Abu'l-Fazl. *Akbar-nāmā* (1596). Trans. Henry Beveridge. 1873. New Delhi: Ess Publications, 1979.

Afaqi, Asadullah. *Shaikh-ul-'Ālam aur Ikiswin Sadī.* Kashmir: Tsrar Sharif, 2003.

——. *T'alimāt-i Shaikhu'l-'Ālam.* 2 vols. Kashmir: Tsrar Sharif, 1998.

Arberry, Arthur J. *Sufism, an account of the Mystics of Islam.* London: Allen & Unwin, 1950.

Bahāristān-i-Shāhī: A Chronicle of Medieval Kashmir. Trans. K.N. Pandit. Calcutta: Firma KLM Private Limited, 1991.

Bamzai, Prithivi N.K. *A History of Kashmir.* Delhi: Metropolitan Book Co., 1962.

Bazaz, Prem Nath. *The History for Struggle for Freedom in Kashmir.* New Delhi. Kashmiri Publishing Co., 1951.

Biscoe, C.E. Tyndale. *Kashmir in Sunlight and Shade.* 1922. Srinagar: Gulshan Publishers, 2005.

Burji Nūr: Hayāt wa Hālāt Shaikh Nūruddīn Nūrāni. 1981. 2nd ed. Srinagar: J&K Academy of Art, Culture & Languages, 1991.

Chatterji, Jagadish C. *Kashmir Shaivism.* Albany. New York: SUNY Press, 1986.

Chittick, William C. *Imaginal Worlds: Ibn al-'Arabī and the Problem of Religious Diversity.* New York: SUNY Press, 1994.

——. *The Self-Disclosure of God: Principles of Ibn al-'Arabī's Cosmology.* New York: SUNY Press, 1998.

——. *The Sufi Path of Knowledge.* New York: SUNY Press, 1989.

——. *The Sufi Path of Love.* New York: SUNY Press, 1983.

Corbin, Henry. *Creative Imagination in the Sufism of Ibn 'Arabi.* Trans. R. Manheim. New Jersey: Princeton University Press, 1969.

Donaldson, Dwight M. *Studies in Muslim Ethics.* London: SPCK Publishing, 1953.

Fox, Warwick. "Deep Ecology: A New Philosophy of our Time." *Environmental Ethics: An Anthology.* Eds. A. Light & H. Rolston III. Oxford: Blackwell Publishing, 2008. 252–261.

Gauhar, G.N. *Sheikh Noor-ud Din Wali* (Nund Rishi). New Delhi: Sahitya Akademi, 1998.

Gems of Kashmiri Literature. Trans. T.N. Kaul. New Delhi: Sanchar Publishing House, 1996.

Green, Nile. *Indian Sufism since the Seventeenth Century*. London & New York: Routledge, 2006.

Grierson, (Sir) George. *A Dictionary of the Kashmiri Language*. 1932. Srinagar: Gulshan Publishers 1999.

Hasan Khuihāmī, P.G. *Tā'rīkih-i-Hasan* (1898). Vols. II & III. Urdu Trans. M. Ibrahim. Srinagar, 1957, 1960.

Hasan, Muhibbu'l. *Kashmir under the Sultans*. Calcutta: Iran Society, 1959.

Husaini, Hayat. A. *The Religious Thought of Mir Saiyid 'Ali Hamadani*. Kashmir: Al-Hamara Publications, 1992.

Ibn 'al Arabī. *Bezels of Wisdom*. Trans. R.W.J. Austin. New Jersey: Paulist Press, 1980.

——. *Meccan Revelations*. Vol. I. Ed. M. Chodkiewicz. Trans. W. Chittick & J. Morris. New York: Pir Press, 2005.

——. *Meccan Revelations*. Vol. II. Ed. M. Chodkiewicz. Trans. C. Chodkiewicz & D. Gril. New York: Pir Press, 2004.

Islamic Path: Sufism, Society and Politics in India. Eds. S. Zaheer, H. Jafri, & H. Reifeld. New Delhi: Rainbow Publishers Ltd., 2006.

Jahangir. *Tūzuk-i-Jahāngīrī*. Trans. A. Rogers and H. Beveridge. 2 vols. New Delhi: Munshiram Manoharlal, 1968.

Jalal, Ayesha. *Self and Sovereignty: Individual and Community in South Asian Islam since 1850*. London and New York: Routledge, 2000.

Jonarāja. *Rājataraṅgiṇī of Jonarāja*. Trans. Jogesh C. Dutt. Delhi: Gian Publishing House, 1986.

Kachru, Braj. *Kashmiri Literature*. Wiesbaden: Otto Harrassowitz, 1981.

Kak, Jaishree. *Mystical Verses of Lallā*. Delhi: Motilal Banarsidass, 2007.

Kalhana. *Rājataraṅgiṇī*. Trans. R.S. Pandit. New Delhi: Sahitya Akademi, 1990.

Kalhana. *Rājataraṅgiṇī*. Trans. M.A. Stein. 2 vols. Delhi: Motilal Banarsidass, 1961.

Kalām-i Shaikh al-'Ālam. Compiled by Mīr Abdullāh. Ms. No. 45, Research and Publication Dept, Srinagar.

Kamāl, Baba. *Nūr-Nāmā* (1802). Ms. No. 726, Oriental Research Department, Srinagar.

——. *Rishī-Nāmā, 'Anbar Shumāmā* (1835). Ms. Nos. 4 & 15, Cultural Academy, Srinagar.

Kamil, M. Amin, ed. *Sufi Shāyir*. 3 Vols. Srinagar: J&K Academy of Art, Culture, & Languages, 1964–65.

Kaul, Advaitavadini. *Buddhist Savants of Kashmir: Their Contribution.* Srinagar: Utpal Publications, 1987.

Kaul, Jaya Lal. *Kashmiri Lyrics.* Srinagar: Rinemisary, 1945.

——. *Lal Ded.* New Delhi: Sahitya Akademi, 1973.

——. *Studies in Kashmiri.* Srinagar: Kapoor Brothers, 1969.

Khākī, Baba Dāwud. *Rishī-Nāmā* (1580–81). Ms. No. 954, Oriental Research Department, Srinagar.

Khalīl, Baba. *Rauzātu'l-Riyāz* (1835). Ms. No. 31, Cultural Academy, Srinagar.

Khan, K.S. Khaja. *Studies in Tasawwuf.* Delhi: Idarah-I Adabiyat-Delli, 1923.

Khan, M. Ishaq. *Kashmir's Transition to Islam.* 1994. 4th ed. Srinagar: Gulshan Books, 2005.

Knowles, J. Hinton. *A Dictionary of Kashmiri Proverbs and Sayings.* 1885. New Delhi: Asian Educational Services, 1985.

The Koran. Trans. N.J. Dawood. 2nd ed. New York, Penguin Classics, 2004.

Koul, Pandit Anand. "Life Sketch of Laleshwari" & "Lalla Vakyani." *Indian Antiquary.* Vols. L (1921); LIX (1930); LX(1931); LXI (1932); LXII (1933).

——. "A Life of Nand Rishi." *Indian Antiquary.* Vols. LVIII (1929) & LIX (1930).

Koul, Omkar N. *A Dictionary of Kashmiri Proverbs.* 1992. 2nd ed. Delhi: Indian Institute of Language Studies, 2006.

Kulliyāt Abdul Ahad Zargar. Ed. Khursheed A. Zargar. Srinagar: Book Bell, 2007.

Kulliyāt Samad Mir. Ed. Moti Lal Saqi. Srinagar: J&K Academy of Art, Culture & Languages, 2004.

Kulliyāt Shams Faqir. Ed. Afaq Aziz. Srinagar: Nund Rishi Cultural Society, 2002.

Kulliyāt-i Shaikhu'l-'Ālam. Ed. Moti Lal Saqi. Srinagar: J&K Academy of Art, Culture & Languages, 1985.

Lallā-Vākyāni: or The Wise Sayings of Lal Ded. Ed. and trans. Sir George Grierson and Lionell D. Barnett. Monograph Royal Asiatic Society, Vol. XVII, London, 1920.

Lawrence, (Sir) Walter. *The Valley of Kashmir.* 1895. Srinagar: Gulshan Publishers, 2002.

The Literary Heritage of Kashmir. Ed. K.L. Kalla. Delhi: Mittal Publications, 1985.

Mattū, Bahāuddīn. *Rishī-Nāmā* (1832). Ms. Nos. 48, 956, 1041, and 1044, Oriental Research Department, Srinagar; Ms. No. 10, Cultural Academy, Srinagar.

Mishkātī, Baba Dāwud. *Asrāru'l-Abrār* (1652–53). Ms. No. 40, Oriental Research Department, Srinagar.

Mohan, Krishna. *Early Medieval History of Kashmir.* New Delhi: Meharchand Lachhmandas Publications, 1981.

Munawwar, Naji and Shafi Shauq. *Kashur Adbuk Tawarikh.* Srinagar: University of Kashmir, 1992.

Naess, Arne, "The Deep Ecological Movement: Some Philosophical Aspects." *Deep Ecology for the 21st Century.* Ed. G. Sessions. Boston: 1995. 64–84.

Nasīb, Baba. *Rishī-Nāmā* (d. 1631–32). Ms. No. 731, Indian Office Library, Delhi; Ms. No. 25, Oriental Research Department, Srinagar; and Ms. No. 13, Cultural Academy, Srinagar.

Nasr, Seyyed H. *Sufi Essays.* Chicago: ABC International Group, Inc., 1999.

Naudou, Jean. *Buddhists of Kashmir.* Delhi: Agam Kala Prakashan, 1980.

Nicholson, Reynold A. *Studies in Islamic Mysticism.* Cambridge: The University Press, 1921.

Nūr-Nāmā: A Collection of the Sayings of Shaikh Nūru'd-Dīn. Ed. M.A. Kamil. Srinagar: J&K Academy of Art, Culture & Languages, 1966.

Nūri, Abdul-Wahhāb, *Futūhāt-i-Kubravīya* (1748–49). Ms. No. 50, Oriental Research Department, Srinagar.

Odin, Jaishree K. *To the Other Shore: Lallā's Life and Verses.* New Delhi: Vitasta, 1999.

Parimoo, B.N. *The Ascent of Self.* 2nd ed. Delhi: Motilal Banarsidass, 1987.

——. ed. and trans. *Unity in Diversity: Nund Rishī.* Srinagar: J&K Academy of Art, Culture & Languages, 1984.

Parmu, R.K. *History of Muslim Rule in Kashmir,* 1320–1819. Delhi: People's Publishing House, 1969.

Rafiqi, Abdul Q. *Sufism in Kashmir: Fourteenth to the Sixteenth Century.* 1976. Revised ed. Sydney: Goodword Media, 2003.

Rai, Mridu. *Hindu Rulers, Muslim Subjects: Islam, Rights and the History of Kashmir.* Delhi: Permanent Black, 2004.

Rahman, Fazlur. *Islam.* 1966. 2nd ed. Chicago: University of Chicago Press, 2002.

Raina, T.N. *An Anthology of Modern Kashmiri Verse.* Poona: Sangam Press, 1972.

——. *A History of Kashmiri Literature.* 2002. New Delhi: Sahitya Akademi, 2005.

——. *A History of Sufism in India* (1978). Vols. 1 and II. New Delhi: Munshiram Manoharlal Publishers, 2003, 2002.

Robinson, Francis. *Islam and Muslim Society in South Asia*. New Delhi: Oxford University Press, 2000.

Rolston III, Holmes. "Value in Nature and the Nature of Value." *Environmental Ethics: An Anthology*. Eds. A. Light and H. Rolston III. Oxford: Blackwell Publishing, 2008. 143–53.

Roy, Asim. *The Islamic Syncretistic Tradition in Bengal*. New Jersey: Princeton University Press, 1983.

Schimmel, Annemarie. *Islam in the Indian Sub-Continent*. Leiden: E.J. Brill, 1980.

Shah, M. Maroof. "A Metaphysical Approach to Rishism." *'Ālamdar, A Journal of Kashmiri Society and Culture*, 2.2, 2008. 103–20.

Shah, M. Maroof and Manzoor A. Shah. "Environmentalist Dimension of Rishi Thought." *'Ālamdar, A Journal of Kashmiri Society and Culture*, 2.2, 2008. 137–59.

Shah, S. Ikbal. A. *Islamic Sufism* (1933). Delhi: Idarah-I Adabiyat-Delli, 1979.

Shah-Kazemi, Reza. *Paths to Transcendence: Shankara, Ibn Arabi, and Meister Eckhart*. Indiana: World Wisdom Inc, 2006.

Sharda, S.R. *Sufi Thought: Its development in Punjab and its Impact on Punjabi Literature*. New Delhi: Munshiram Manoharlal, 1974.

Shauq, Shafi. "Linguistic Study of the Shruk." *'Ālamdar: A Journal of Kashmiri Society and Culture*, Vol. II, No. 2, 2008.

Singer, Peter. "Not for Humans Only: The Place of Nonhumans in Environmental Issues." *Environmental Ethics: An Anthology*. Eds. A. Light and H. Rolston III. Oxford: Blackwell Publishing, 2008. 55–64.

Sufi, G.M.D. *Kashir: A History of Kashmir*. 2 vols. New Delhi: Light and Life Publishers, 1974.

——. *Islamic Culture in Kashmir*. New Delhi: Light and Life Publishers, 1979.

Sufi Shāyir. Ed. M. Amin Kamil. 3 vols. Srinagar: J&K Academy of Art, Culture, and Languages, 1964–65.

Taylor, Paul W. "The Ethics of Respect for Nature." *Environmental Ethics: An Anthology*. Eds. A. Light and H. Rolston III, Oxford: Blackwell Publishing, 2008. 74–84.

Temple, Richard C. *The Religion and Teachings of Lalla* (1924). New Delhi: Vintage Books, 1990.

The Koran. Trans. N.J. Dawood. 2nd edn. New York: Penguin Classics, 2004.

The Literary Heritage of Kashmir. Ed. K.L. Kalla. Delhi: Mittal Publications, 1985.

Tickoo, J.L. *Kashmiri-English Dictionary*. Delhi: Indian Institute of Language Studies, 2006.

Tikku, G.L. "Mysticism in Kashmir: In the Fourteenth and Fifteenth Centuries." *Muslim World*, LIII, July 1963. 226–33.

Unity in Diversity: Nund Rishi. Ed. and trans. B.N. Parimoo. Srinagar: J&K Academy of Art, Culture and Languages, 1984.

Valiuddin, Mir. *The Quranic Sufism* (1959). Delhi: Motilal Banarsidass, 2002.

Wani, M. Ashraf. *Islam in Kashmir: Fourteenth to Sixteenth Century*. Srinagar: Oriental Publishing House, 2004.

Zafar, Sayyadah A. *Saiyyid Mir Ali Hamadani*. Srinagar: Gulshan Publishers, 1991.

Zutshi, Chitralekha. *Languages of Belonging: Islam, Regional Identity and the Making of Kashmir*. Delhi: Permanent Black, 2003.

Index